Fearfully and Wonderfully Made

Liz Williams

Table of Contents

Dedication

This book is dedicated to Lucas and Ava, the catalysts to my healing.

Acknowledgment

A special thanks to my husband Matt for his unwavering love and support in the writing of this book.

About the Author

Liz Williams lives in South Carolina with her husband Matt, children Lucas (4) and Ava (2), and her Mini-Bernedoodle, Rex. In her free time, she enjoys yoga, running, photography, and losing herself in a good book. She strives to be a servant of God and a conduit for his message.

Page Left Blank Intentionally

Introduction

"I praise you, for I am fearfully and wonderfully made. Your works are wonderful, I know that full well."

— Psalm 139:14 NIV

Forty is a profound milestone in one's life. As I approach my fortieth birthday, I aim to free myself from mental slavery. This book serves as a journal of my experience in discovering my authentic purpose ordained by God, my Christian Testimony.

The number forty is repeatedly used in the Bible to refer to a period of trial and struggle.

I.   Jesus was tempted in the desert by the devil for forty days:

"[1]Then Jesus was led by the Spirit into the wilderness to be tempted by the devil. [2]After fasting forty days and forty nights, he was hungry. [3]The tempter came to him and said, 'If you are the Son of God, tell these stones to become bread.' [4]Jesus answered, 'It is written: Man shall not live on bread alone, but on every word that comes from the mouth of God.'"

— Mathew 4: 1–4

II. Moses led the Israelites out of slavery after forty years:

"[30]After forty years had passed, an angel appeared to Moses in the flames of a burning bush in the desert near Mount Sinai. [31]When he saw this, he was amazed at the sight. As he went over to get a closer

look, he heard the Lord say: ^{32} 'I am the God of your fathers, the God of Abraham, Isaac and Jacob.' Moses trembled with fear and did not dare to look."

— **Acts 7: 30-32**

III. The Great Flood lasted for forty days:

"^{17}For forty days, the flood kept coming on the earth, and as the waters increased, they lifted the ark high above the earth. ^{18}The waters rose and increased greatly on the earth, and the ark floated on the surface of the water."

— **Genesis 7: 17-18**

This book is divided into three parts reflecting my life into three stages — Childhood, Early Adult Hood, and Motherhood, each of which was giving me different tests of my faith and resilience. At each stage, I confronted obstacles that tested me to grow in spirit.

The fourth part of the book deals with practices and tools that have helped me out in shaping my faith journey. These insights are personal and seek to offer others helpful approaches to tackling their challenges.

It was at thirty-nine that I had what must be described as my own great flood when all of the tears that I'd carried with me throughout my life began to gush out. It emerged in this respect at least as a watershed in my own personal and spiritual development, and it forms in itself a strand running through this story of endurance, belief, and recovery.

6

Part I: Childhood — 0-18 Years

"²²But the fruit of the Spirit is love, joy, peace, forbearance, kindness, goodness, faithfulness, ²³gentleness and self-control. Against such things, there is no law. ²⁴Those who belong to Christ Jesus have crucified the flesh with its passions and desires. ²⁵Since we live by the Spirit, let us keep in step with the Spirit."

— Galatians 5:22-25 NIV

The love story between a father and daughter is sacred and ordained by God. A father is his daughter's physical representation of God. He is omniscient and omnipotent. Her relationship with her father informs her entire sense of self. Her value system, self-esteem, self-worth, and authenticity are all heavily influenced by him. He serves as her guiding light and moral compass.

My father is 6'2" and two hundred forty pounds. He is terrifying in stature and spirit. He provided a minuscule amount of affection. And he rarely smiled. I had to become an expert in the subtle shifts in facial expressions as a survival mechanism. He had a very short fuse, and the smallest shift in my behavior would set him off. Most days, when he got home from work, he would go down to the basement to play his computer games. Occasionally, however, he would wrap me up like a burrito in a blanket and tickle me. My body would tense up when he touched me; his nails would dig into my skin with a force and pressure that was uncomfortable. I did not deem it safe to voice my discomfort and silently endured.

My father's first love was himself; his second love was power, and his third love was music. Music was our love language. It allowed us to communicate in ways that were limited by the spoken word. Music is spiritual, creative, evocative, expressive, free — all the things my father was not. He had no creative energy and was infinitely jealous of those who possessed those talents.

The one and only gift my father gave me was a love for music, and it kept me alive. My identity is locked away in the songs of my childhood. As I go back and make sense of my story, the songs I listened to will hold many insights. Music was my escape during my childhood; it helped me regulate my emotions and connect with the larger humanity safely. I was curious about the impact of music, and some quick research confirmed that it has many benefits, including the ability to give energy, soothe the heart, fight depression, enhance creativity, reduce physiological pain, release dopamine, and enhance memory. My memories stay locked in the rhythm and melodies and will help me understand who I am as I reconnect with my authentic self. As I reacquaint myself with these songs, I will find that the songs I was drawn to were speaking to my subconscious all along.

I have always been fascinated by abnormal psychology. Growing up, I watched Alfred Hitchcock films, Scream, Halloween, The Exorcist, The Blair Witch Project, and any other thriller movie I could find. As documentaries became more popular, I ventured into serial documentaries on John Wayne Gacy, Ted Bundy, etc. I wanted to understand what happened to someone to get them to the point where they had no empathy for another human being and could consciously harm them with no remorse. After the video or documentary was over, I would research the subject afterward, trying to solve the puzzle of WHY.

My father abused me physically, emotionally, and sexually before I could speak. Any "mistake" had a penance and price to pay. His goal was to slowly and systematically break my spirit, day by day. Each day was a battle: Would I give in to my sinful nature, or would I appeal to my angelic side? Men have used the sacred spiritual energy and femininity of women to shame us for centuries; it's one of the men's greatest hits.

The physical abuse stopped by the time my hippocampus formed around the age of four. As an elementary school teacher, my father was well-versed in psychology, particularly that of child development, and he made this known. He would frequently spout out psychological terms like projection, displacement, positive reinforcement, and punishment. He was well-versed in the power of psychological manipulation. The hippocampus is important to my story because this brain region is responsible for memory, learning, and emotions.

My mother was psychologically brainwashed by the time I was born. She was unable to give birth to me vaginally and was in labor with me for over a day before being scheduled for a C-section. The hips are the area where we, as women, store sexual trauma, so that makes complete sense to me now. I can only imagine the sexual trauma that she went through under my father's hand prior to my birth.

Religion was a cornerstone of my childhood. I grew up going to the local Presbyterian church with my mom and brother most Sundays. My father never went to church with us, and his excuse was that he went to church for his entire childhood and knew everything that he needed to know. I found this odd but internalized that my father was exempt from the rules and expectations that applied to the rest of us; he was "special" and above religious law.

I am a dreamer by nature — an idealist. My father knew this and would appeal to this side of me when it was beneficial for him, particularly in his musical choices. He knew I was a feminist and was a strong advocate for women's rights from a young age so he would select songs written by women as a way to influence my worldview while growing up. I was also inspired by nature as it reminded me of God's limitless power in creation. My father had pictures of his photography scattered throughout the house.

My father made his superior status clear to me on our trips in the car together. One of his favorite songs was Tom Petty's "*Free Fallin'*," a song about breaking a girl's heart without guilt or remorse:

She's a good girl
Loves her Mama
Loves Jesus
And America Too
And I'm a bad boy because I don't even miss her
I'm a bad boy for breaking her heart

My dad would take me to Grand Rapids with him to go to the gaming store. On the drive up, we would listen to music, the soundtrack of our relationship. My father told me this was our special time and that our relationship was special — nobody else would understand. The lyrics of the songs became the moral law that I was expected to live by. My goal as a Christian woman was to be a good girl and follow the established rules. I internalized that these rules did not apply to my father. My prize for going along on the hour-long trip was a visit to Toys' R Us. The pure joy of walking through the aisles under the bright fluorescent lights hit my dopamine circuits deep. The possibilities were endless; the world was my oyster.

We would listen to Bruce Springsteen, Tom Petty, and The Police together, letting the emotions of the music hit us while silently enjoying it between his lectures. Intermittently, my dad would look in the rearview mirror with his piercing blue eyes, communicating that these songs were an unwritten code that I was supposed to follow. My job was to be obedient, well-behaved, and faithful. The same rules did not apply to him; he had free rein to live his life as he deemed fit.

He told me that he got into teaching because he was a shy child and wanted to perfect his public speaking. He projected himself as a perfectionist because he knew early on that I had perfectionist tendencies. On some level, children were his emotional peers. It was also a profession that had an air of legitimacy and was a respected position in the community.

Another one of my father's favorites was The Police's "Every Breath You Take," a classic but also creepy song about a man stalking a woman:

Every breath you take

And every move you make

Every bond you break

Every step you take

I'll be watching you

Every single day

And every word you say

Every game you play

Every night you stay

I'll be watching you

Oh, can't you see

You belong to me?

How my poor heart aches

With every step you take?

He made sure that I knew he was omniscient and omnipotent, Every move I made was under surveillance. Every decision was scrutinized and had to be answered for; every transgression had a consequence.

I had an insatiable curiosity about the world that my father used for his benefit. He reminded me incessantly about the evil of Eve in her pursuit of knowledge. Women were responsible for the downfall in Eden and the Original Sin of mankind. Any worldly behavior normal for a young girl was proof that I was an evil temptress. To make up for this sin, a woman had to be subservient, quiet and selfless, a penance held throughout the Old Testament.

My father would make disparaging comments about my friendships. Any of my friends who brought me closer to my authentic self were *troubling, too proud,* or *negative.* He was extremely careful about the outside influence of others to ensure that I remained voiceless in every aspect of my life. My hands were abused to prevent me from making an account of my abuse. My mouth was degraded to prevent me from speaking out. My ribs were covered with sin to prevent me from taking in a full breath.

Eve was formed out of man in **Genesis 2: 20-23**:

[20]So the man gave names to all the livestock, the birds in the sky, and all the wild animals. But for Adam, no suitable helper was found. [21]So the Lord God caused the man to fall into a deep sleep, and while he was sleeping, he took one of the man's ribs and then closed up the place with flesh. [22]Then the Lord God made a woman from the rib he had taken out of the man, and he brought her to the man. [23]The man said, 'This is now bone of my bones and flesh of my flesh; she shall be called 'woman,' for she was taken out of man.'"

The human spirit is incredibly powerful. Through the abuse, I still found opportunities to self-soothe and ground myself. I walked barefoot incessantly. I took time to splash in puddles with my rain boots during thunderstorms. I covered up my trembling with a blanket to give myself the hug I desperately wanted but never received from my parents. I climbed trees and felt the healing presence of the wind; I can still see the lush green, yellow, and red leaves, reminding me of God's promise that every time, there is a season. I knew that this pain would not last forever.

As is said in **Ecclesiastes 3: 1-8**:

"¹There is a time for everything, and a season for every activity under the heavens: ²a time to be born and a time to die, a time to plant and a time to uproot, ³a time to kill and a time to heal, a time to tear down and a time to build, ⁴a time to weep and a time to laugh, a time to mourn and a time to dance, ⁵a time to scatter stones and a time to gather them, a time to embrace and a time to refrain from embracing, ⁶a time to search and a time to give up, a time to keep and a time to throw away, ⁷a time to tear and a time to mend, a time to be silent and a time to speak, ⁸a time to love and a time to hate, a time for war and a time for peace."

I love rainstorms. I have incredibly fond memories of splashing in puddles with my rain boots and raincoat, spinning around, and dancing with my arms outstretched. It was a reminder that God would make good on His word. A rainbow served as a reminder of God's promise to me in **Genesis 9:12-16**:

"¹²And God said, "This is the sign of the covenant I am making between me and you, and every living creature with you, a covenant for all generations to come:¹³I have set my rainbow in the clouds, and it will be the sign of the covenant between me and the earth.¹⁴Whenever I bring clouds over the earth and the rainbow appears in the clouds. ¹⁵I will remember my covenant between me and

you and all living creatures of every kind. Never again will the waters become a flood to destroy all life. [16]*Whenever the rainbow appears in the clouds, I will see it and remember the everlasting covenant between God and all living creatures of every kind on the earth."*

One of my earliest memories is that of my grandfather, my dad's father. I have an incredibly heavy feeling in my chest and a tender spot in my heart. I am not sure if my memories of my grandfather are dreams or reality. One image that floods me is falling asleep in his arms in a small, worn-out wooden chair on his deck overlooking the Lake Michigan sunset. I was cradled and safe. I was loved without any conditions. I was cared for. My human needs for connection and physical touch were met. It was a moment of sheer perfection.

Another of my first memories was eating Burger King chicken nuggets with my mother's parents while my parents were in the hospital, awaiting my brother's birth. My brother was born in November, shortly before I turned four. I was with my mother's parents at a family member's condo in Grand Rapids. I remember them receiving a phone call from the hospital that there were complications with the birth and that my brother had pneumonia. My grandmother was extremely anxious, so I'm sure I picked up on her panic. Our family was in crisis, and my mother and father were far away.

When I think of my grandfather, I can feel the brokenness of my heart that my four-year-old self felt as I saw his dead body in the open casket at his visitation. I cannot remember if I screamed or cried, but I knew that the world was no longer safe. My body now convulses, and I cry the guttural sobs of a child lacking self-consciousness. I must have been incredibly confused and scared. At four years old, I was too young to grasp the concept of death, and little was done to explain it to me. The world no longer made sense and was not safe. I lacked the language to articulate how I felt. The concept of death was not something my little brain could comprehend. I asked my mother why Grandpa's body was here, but his eyes were closed, and he was not talking.

"His soul went to heaven," she said.

I knew my family was fundamentally different that day. If I could just be perfect, maybe I could fix us. Like Humpty Dumpty, we had a great fall.

Growing up, I had a recurring dream that my grandfather was alive. During the dream, we were on the Lake Michigan beach, feeding seagulls, running after each other, holding hands, and laughing. I remember the sheer panic and sorrow I felt when I awoke and reality set in that he was dead.

My father and his brother were in a constant battle for the patriarch role of the family. My grandmother lived about twenty minutes away, and we would see her each Sunday at her house on the Lake Michigan coast. She cooked us pizza with Chef Boyardee sauce. During dinner, my father would relay the accomplishments of the week. It was very performative, and I felt early on that I needed to play my part. My grades were a constant topic of conversation.

My grandmother was extremely cold, unloving, and unsettling. She had an air of superiority as if we were boring her with the details of our lives. I learned very quickly to keep my head down and keep to myself.

I have a few memories of my grandmother's wrath. When I was around six years old she went into a rage because I climbed up the stairs. Upstairs was forbidden for all the grandchildren. Subconsciously, I wanted to connect with my grandfather who passed away, hoping that he might be up there. My memory believes that I had pleasant memories with him upstairs before he became sick.

Another time, I got chastised for trying to pat her Sheltie Sammy while she was eating her lunch. Sammy bit me, and my grandmother was irritated that I was too stupid to know that dogs do not like to be bothered during this time. I had broken the moral law.

When I was around three or four years old I took dance and gymnastics classes. This was a threat to my father; my ability to express myself in an authentic way through my body was used against me as the evil temptress Eve, responsible for tempting men into all kinds of sin. He made sure to tell me how fat I looked in my leotard to induce shame within me. If I was the scapegoat for all his toxic shame, he was wiped clean of any shame of his own.

I would find secret opportunities to dance in my room by myself, away from his grasp. Eventually, though, I stopped taking classes as I became overly self-conscious of my body — already deep in shame.

His goal was to make me as worldly as possible so that I would stay in my sin and shame.

As is stated in **Genesis 3**:

"¹Now the serpent was more crafty than any of the wild animals the Lord God had made. He said to the woman, 'Did God really say, 'You must not eat from any tree in the garden'?' ²The woman said to the serpent, We may eat fruit from the trees in the garden,³but God did say, 'You must not eat fruit from the tree that is in the middle of the garden, and you must not touch it, or you will die.'⁴'You will not certainly die,' the serpent said to the woman.⁵'For God knows that when you eat from it your eyes will be opened, and you will be like God, knowing good and evil.'⁶When the woman saw that the fruit of the tree was good for food and pleasing to the eye, and also desirable for gaining wisdom, she took some and ate it. She also gave some to her husband, who was with her, and he ate it.⁷Then the eyes of both of them were opened, and they realized they were naked; so they sewed fig leaves together and made coverings for themselves."

My feelings were also invalidated by the outside world. I was at my friend Rachel's birthday party when I was around five years old. There was heavy suction at the bottom of the pool and I was fluttering underwater, drawn in by the suction. Someone jumped in and pulled me out. I had a panic attack, gasping for air. The adult who pulled me out invalidated my fear and feelings.

My mother's parents treated me with love and kindness. I felt safe and cared for in their presence. I have memories of building gingerbread houses with my grandfather during the holidays. My grandmother would take me on nature walks. Every spring, she would point out all of the flowers that were blooming. He would let me ride with him on his riding lawn mower when he mowed the grass. My grandfather would explain all of the vegetables growing in their garden. My grandmother would make homemade bread for us as a special treat. When we spent the night at their house, we would wake up to Raisin Bran and watch Sesame Street on their tiny TV in the morning. My brother and I would play in the creek by their house, catching frogs or exploring the woods behind their home. Nature was my way to ground myself and connect with God's beautiful creation.

My father loved to humiliate me socially under the guise of teasing. I always left the interaction deflated and feeling terrible about myself. I used to blush terribly — our bodies' first sign of shame. The subject of conversation was irrelevant; the goal was for me to feel degraded and ashamed. This was only exacerbated when I was told that I needed to toughen up if I tried to say that my feelings were hurt. I was taught very early to shove my feelings down and ignore my gut instincts. My intuition was slowly and systematically annihilated; my inner voice could not be trusted.

When I was around seven or eight I have a distinct memory of praying to God that I would go to heaven in case I was killed in the middle of the night. I remember lying in my bed in survival mode because I heard my father's footsteps in the hallway.

My dad had a God complex. I remember calling him "Daddy" once; he got visibly enraged. I was not his daughter; I was his slave. I dressed up as a princess at the age of eight for Halloween. When I was asked about my need for a prince, I said, "I don't need a prince charming!" Even then, I knew that a man who wanted to save a woman was typically a wolf in sheep's clothing and could not be trusted.

My father wore just his underwear to bed and walked around only in his underwear. I remember one time seeing him naked when he got out of the shower and getting a feeling that I had seen him naked before.; it was an eerie, disorienting feeling.

My father would abuse me at night. In psychological terms, the unconscious is associated with the night. The shadow is the part of us that lurks beneath the surface. His elixir of abuse was cough syrup. Anytime he heard me cough, he would overdose me and pick me up in the middle of the night. In my transfixed state, he would carry me to his dungeon — our family basement. My sleep deprivation impacted my performance at school, which only led to more shame.

Whenever we played anything competitive as a family, my dad had to win. My mom would get angry and say, "Why can't you let the kids win?" My dad would respond, "I am trying to teach them a lesson." Typically, I would team up with my father, while my brother teamed up with my mother for family games. My father made it clear that he was disappointed in me if I got an answer wrong or did not perform as expected. He would pout like a five-year-old boy if we lost at a game.

Feelings were an inconvenient nuisance for my father. I cannot remember how many times I was told, "You are too sensitive" or "Life isn't fair," rather than having my experience validated. Eventually, I started to believe him. When I questioned this train of thought, I was

disrespectful and told that I needed to "honor thy father and mother" —
an effective manipulation tactic derived from one of the Ten
Commandments in our religious family.

My body was a reminder that I was not perfect. In second grade,
one of my classmates told me I was fat after we were weighed in the
classroom. In my toxic shame, I internalized this comment, and it played
on repeat in my head anytime I wanted to eat something unhealthy. I
started to diet in second grade; my body became my enemy, and its day-
to-day needs were ignored.

I also received some less-than-perfect grades that year. Although I
cannot remember what was said to me, it must have been internalized
as a character flaw. Our grading system in second grade went from 1 to
3, with 1 being the highest mark. After receiving a few 2s, my father
would not let me hear the end of it. I asked one of my babysitters to
create addition and subtraction tables for me as a "fun" activity.

My life forever changed one Sunday night while driving back from
my grandmother's house. We borrowed her Jeep because our car was in
the shop for repairs. We had the sunroof open and windows down; it
was right before sunset, and I had my arm outside the window enjoying
the beautiful breeze. The next thing I knew, my father and I were upside
down in our seatbelts, skidding on the pavement.

"Are you okay?" he asked.

People in the residential area came out of their houses to check on
us. We were asked if we wanted an ambulance, but my dad said that it
was not necessary because we couldn't afford it — another subtle

reminder that I was not worth care — and oh, a not-so-subtle reminder that he had power over life and death.

I'm sure I was blamed for the accident in some way.

I saw the sign

And it opened up my eyes, I saw the sign

Life is demanding without understanding

I saw the sign

And it opened up my eyes, I saw the sign

And no one's gonna drag you up to get into the light where you belong

But where do you belong? Oh, oh, oh

— The Sign "Ace of Base"

My father gave me his old radio for second grade and I started listening to popular radio in our basement. This was when dance music became very popular. I was obsessed with Ace of Base's "I Saw the Sign." My dad had plenty of commentary on my taste in music, claiming it was far inferior to his. I relished my ability to pick what I liked. I would record songs on the radio with a blank tape and play them back.

My father had an intense interest in technology, and we were fortunate to have all of the latest video game systems. This was where the intermittent reinforcement came in. He made it seem like these gifts were for us, but my father wanted the systems for himself. He had a severe shopping addiction, and his habits were not supported by his teacher's salary. I had a Neo Geo, Sega Genesis, Super Nintendo, PlayStation, Nintendo 64, Dreamcast, you name it. Playing video games was a bonding experience between my brother and me. Our favorite games to play together were Donkey Kong and Banjo Kazooie. The complexities of life faded away when we could align against a common goal of defeating the bad guy in front of us on the screen.

I was the oldest grandchild on my father's side of the family, and it was made clear to me that I was the designated caretaker. My cousin Michael was three years younger, my brother was four years younger, and my cousin Katie was five years younger. We would spend holidays playing shuffleboard in the basement, playing Super Nintendo's Donkey Kong, and climbing up the swing set. I remember getting shamed and belittled one time when one of my cousins went upstairs — an area that was off-limits to the kids. "How could you let this happen?" I was responsible not only for myself but also for other children with their own free will. I was not performing my role perfectly and it was made known.

Test-taking was always an opportunity to prove or disprove my worth. My babysitter moved on to multiplication tables for me as I entered third grade. My anxiety would shoot through the roof, and panic would set in. I remember the feeling of disappointment when another kid would finish the timed tests before me. I was deep in survival mode.

Christmas in fourth grade, I brought my first cassette tape from my father's sister, Ginny, for my Walkman. The album was Hootie and the Blowfish's Cracked Rear View and I was obsessed. This was my first independent musical interest. I remember my father criticizing the quality of this music, but I did not care. I could put my headphones in and tune him out, and I did so regularly.

I learned about molestation in fourth grade. I looked the word up in the dictionary; "*molest*" meant to pester — the definition did not fit my situation. Nevertheless, I made a complaint to my teacher that my father was molesting me. I remember the song "Sunny Came Home" by Shawn Colvin that details abuse:

Sunny came home to her favorite room

Sunny sat down in the kitchen

She opened a book and a box of tools

Sunny came home with a mission

She says, "Days go by, I'm hypnotized

I'm walking on a wire

I close my eyes and fly out of my mind

Into the fire"

Sunny came home with a list of names

She didn't believe in transcendence

"And it's time for a few small repairs," she said

Sunny came home with a vengeance

She says, "Days go by, I don't know why

I'm walking on a wire

I close my eyes and fly out of my mind

Into the fire"

I made a complaint against my father to my teacher. When my father found out, he turned into an absolute monster and told me that if

I ever tried to use my voice, he would kill my entire family and burn our house down. This was yet another way to silence me and take my voice away.

I always wore a t-shirt over my bathing suit and baggy clothes. During that time, I thought this was related to being self-conscious about my body — which was true — but there was something deeper. I knew my father looked at me like a predator, which really creeped me out. I felt like a piece of delicious meat to his disturbed mind.

To make things right with the teacher, he provided me with child labor the next year. My father moved to another school for a gifted and talented program, and I transitioned from third to fifth grade. I helped him in his classroom all day when I was in sixth grade to smooth over the waters and keep the school off his tracks.

My sickness was an inconvenience and not consistent with his self-centered agenda. Anytime I was sick from school, I was required to go to the doctor; he made it clear that something better was wrong with me. I also knew that I would be weighed at the doctor's office, which carried its own shame.

One day in fourth grade, I felt extremely nauseous all day but tried to will it out of my body because we had a school field trip that day to listen to some African dance music. I kept it together throughout the whole presentation but threw up in the bathroom right before we took the bus home. I had to sit at the front of the bus by myself, subject to the shaming stares of my classmates — so close but not quite perfect — and once again, my body failed me.

When we saw my grandmother that week, my mom told her that when asked why I did not tell anyone at school that I wasn't feeling well, I said that I needed to be a "strong woman." They laughed it off. Looking back, this is heartbreaking to remember.

One of the Bible songs I remember clearly is "This Little Light of Mine." This song was my anthem during my elementary school years.

This little light of mine

I'm going to let it shine

Oh, this little light of mine

I'm going to let it shine

This little light of mine

I'm going to let it shine

Let it shine, all the time, let it shine

All around the neighborhood

I'm going to let it shine

All around the neighborhood

I'm going to let it shine

All around the neighborhood

When I was around ten years old, my mother gave me the sex talk. She explained how this worked, and I remember feeling completely appalled. I knew at that point that my father had violated my most sacred intimacy. As a person full of toxic shame, I internalized this and held myself responsible for the unspeakable acts that I was forced into. Toxic shame can take over your entire personality; your identity is a summation of the terrible things done to you. My only resolution to avoid this toxic shame was to be perfect — an endeavor I spent thirty-nine years chasing.

My religious upbringing made the talk of sex shameful. When my mom gave me the "sex talk," she was extremely uncomfortable. Discomfort was associated with being unsafe, so I asked limited questions about my changing body. This was extremely disorienting.

Time why you punish me

Like a wave bashing into the shore

You wash away my dreams

Time why you walk away

Like a friend with somewhere to go

You left me crying

Can you teach me 'bout tomorrow

And all the pain and sorrow running free

'Cause tomorrow's just another day

And I don't believe in time

— "Time," Hootie and the Blowfish

My life changed forever during a Camp Geneva trip in the summer between fourth and fifth grade. I asked Jesus Christ into my heart during a daily devotional. The Holy Spirit was now protecting me against the wickedness of the world and my temporary circumstances. One of my favorite Bible verses during this time was:

"Your Word is a lamp for my feet a light on my path."

— Psalm 119:105

My mother is a godly woman, and I used this as an opportunity to show my father that his evil intentions would not win in the end. Satan is known as the Lord of the Flies for his incessant nature to bug and tempt us into sin. One of my favorite songs was "*Shoo Fly Don't Bother Me.*" My brother and I would watch Disney movies together and laugh incessantly when the evil villain was put in their place and lost in the battle of good versus evil. Our favorite movie growing up was The Lion King, and we laughed and danced when Scar fell to his death.

I was the superhero of the family; I needed to be for my survival. I was my father's wife and therapist, my mother's therapist, and my brother's parent. We watched the cartoon Mighty Mouse, and I internalized his motto: "Here I come to save the day!" I was not allowed to have authentic needs. Needs were a threat to my survival and were repressed. All self-esteem and self-worth I had came from swooping in to cheer my family up in times of distress. I became addicted to the dopamine rush of solving my family's problems.

As with any skilled abuser, my father used intermittent reinforcement to keep my family stuck in the cycle of abuse. Not all my memories were negative. I had some fond moments with him. We went on family vacations each summer while my dad was off from teaching. We traveled all over the country — Upper Peninsula of Michigan, Mall of America in Minnesota, New York, New Jersey, Rocky Mountains in Colorado, and Yosemite National Forest in California.

I also knew that I could escape the abuse by hiding from my father. I would hide in bushes, climb trees, find peace in our pine tree, ride my bike through the neighborhood, and spend time at my best friend's house — anything that kept me away from his evil grasp.

When I hit middle school, I had to navigate the unwritten rules and expectations of teenage girls with limited assistance. My father's sister told me that she never shaved above the knee. My mother had very little makeup and did not know how to apply it. My father did not want me to wear any makeup, but my mother convinced him to let me wear a limited supply. I figured it out through trial and error.

My father was home during the summer with my brother and me. When I hit fifth grade, we stopped going to a babysitter's house during the summer; I became the mother of the house. I was responsible for determining our lunch — frozen pizza, SpaghettiOs, or macaroni & cheese. My father never raised a finger. I was also expected to load the dishwasher, clean up the house, do dishes, and vacuum before my mother got home around 3:00 pm. By this age, I could sense that my mother was very unhappy, and this was a way to cheer her up. My father's only household chores were mowing the lawn and taking out the garbage.

My dad had a habit of shaming me in front of people to make sure I knew he was in control. He always said he was teasing, but there was a bite to it that felt humiliating. One time he told his entire third-grade class that I took my first shower that day. When I saw some of these kids during summer break, they made sure to inform me about it. He made me perform dances from elementary school in front of my whole family without ever asking if I wanted to perform them. Everything with his family was a performance, and I needed to stay in character.

I tried to confide in my mother about my abuse, which only led to more shame. I would tell her that I did not believe my father loved me. Her response was always, "Your father loves you; he just has a different way of showing it." This was the narrative while he would degrade her about her weight regularly, telling her she should exercise, wear makeup, get some contacts, or buy some nicer clothes. He would make comments about being very attracted to redheads, even though my mother had brown hair. He never cooked, never cleaned, and rarely assisted with homework. My mother bought her own birthday and Christmas presents, and I wrapped them. Love was full of conditions.

He used to bring me into his computer room with him while he played Diablo. He would sit me on his lap and place his hand on my thigh. I'm sure he loved the feeling of absolute fear when he felt me tense up. He would "accidentally" walk in on me in the bathroom. I eventually started locking the door. He would barge into the bathroom when I took a shower to use the restroom. It was incredibly creepy and unsettling. I existed for his every need.

My fourth-grade teacher, Ms. Rypma, a more free-spirited animal lover, made me feel seen and heard. She was a friend of our family and had a connection with one of my grandmother's close friends. I became more vocal in the classroom; I raised my hand more freely and spoke with a larger group of friends. I also played soccer that year with several girls at my school. Ms. Rypma noted on one of my report cards that I was coming out of my shy "shell." I remember sobbing one day when I had to sit out in the hall for talking too much. The shame of disappointing her was overwhelming. She took an intense liking to me and made me feel seen, felt, and heard.

I somehow knew that God lived in me and that Jesus would triumph in the end. I learned tactics about how to stop an evil trance. As a super empath, I can connect with and feel people's energy; I can literally feel energy and get sucked into it. My coping mechanism as a child was to snap my fingers to break the energy.

There were tender reminders of God's presence. The overwhelming beauty of the Lake Michigan sunset comforted me during my loneliness. I loved the feeling of the cold sand between my toes and the calming, refreshing comfort of the cold water enveloping my body like the hug I always wanted.

My brother and I loved Nickelodeon's SNICK program on Saturday nights. One of our favorites was All That, a sketch comedy show like Saturday Night Live. TLC performed Creep one evening on the show while my brother and I did backflips off the couch in our sunroom.

Through all the trauma, my human spirit prevailed. I walked around barefoot to ground myself; the feeling of the grass on my feet reminded me that I was God's child. I kept a blanket on me to give myself the hug and comfort I so dearly lacked. I climbed a tree for safety and found shelter underneath one of the four large oak trees in the yard.

Adolescence: Lizzie

Over time, I became very tense in social situations due to conditioning dynamics. My body would perspire, and I used self-deprecating humor as a defense mechanism to point out my flaws before anyone else could shame me. This was my mode of operation up until my late thirties.

I remember my brother's birthday presents more than my own growing up. Looking back, I'm sure this was intentional. My father enjoyed seeing the resentment and anger I felt, knowing that my brother received a better gift than I did. This was also a tactic to create discord between the two of us. Nothing made my father happier than inflicting pain on my brother, mother, and me.

In ninth grade, I took an acting class to "perfect" my acting skills. My teacher noted regularly that I had extremely animated facial expressions. My face, like the rest of my body, is very expressive. I would betray my true intentions, which would ramp up my abuse. This was another silencing technique that worked throughout high school.

During my limited social interaction with family members outside of my immediate family, he would make sure to walk up and assert his dominance when I spoke with anyone one-on-one. His piercing eye contact would terrify me each time. This was a not-so-subtle control move.

All of my fears growing up were representations of my terror of my father. I had a recurring dream about an evil kangaroo. I remember waking my mom up in the middle of the night and asking if I could sleep with her. I was terrified of spiders to the point that they would make my skin crawl. I remember my dad forcing me to watch Arachnophobia when I was a teenager as a way of "facing my fear," sadistically laughing while I was terrified. Looking back, my fear of spiders was based on the fact that I felt like prey my entire childhood, caught in my father's web that seemed impossible to escape.

I fell in love with Colorado after our family trip. As I neared graduation I started researching the cost of out-of-state college programs. My father made it clear that the out-of-state tuition was too expensive. As a traumatized child, that option was out of the question. My role was to be submissive.

My subconscious was telling me that I needed to get away. I had a recurring dream about flying. I can remember the feeling of weightlessness, pure joy, and freedom. Once I received my driver's license, I would go for drives regularly at night. I was terrified of driving but more terrified of being near him. I loved driving with the windows down and feeling the breeze hit my face and body.

My reality was so traumatizing and deprived of love and affection that I took on a feeling of limerence, where I actually had to create a fantasy world. I was obsessed with Grant Hill and seriously thought that I was going to marry him. In sixth grade, I completed a book report on him and dressed up like him in his Detroit Pistons jersey for my presentation. I watched every game I was able to, and if the game was on television, I would listen to it on the radio. I watched the games with my parents. When he was traded from the Detroit Pistons to the Orlando Magic in ninth grade, I was absolutely devastated. It made sense; my intricate fantasy world came crashing down.

Discord was so intoxicating to my father. He knew I was insecure about my body, so he took every opportunity to shame me. "Are you sure you want to eat that?" "Put some clothes on!" I remember him telling me that I needed to start wearing deodorant at the age of ten, "You smell terrible!" No guidance was provided; once again, I had to navigate the waters on my own through trial and error. He would make side glances at my body, noting his disgust. I developed an eating disorder at the age of ten due to body shaming from my father, and then he would gaslight me and say, "Hey, skinny bones! You're so thin." It was a psychological hell. My individualism was systematically destroyed — a slow death by a thousand cuts.

At some point during my teenage years, I realized that I needed to put on my best acting performance during each social experience. I could feel the moment when I dissociated from my spirit and became a robotic shell of myself. This came up most frequently when we would go to my grandmother's house each Sunday. I had to present the perfect daughter image to my grandmother, aunt, and family friends. My spirit slowly dimmed with each exchange.

He wanted to recreate his childhood loneliness in me. I was incredibly isolated, a common abuse tactic. If I had a friend come over, he would make sure to let me know that they said something about me or sabotaged the relationship. He controlled every aspect of my worldview. If I could not speak with anyone or share my experience, how could I understand how utterly depraved this situation was?

When I turned twelve, I started developing chronic tickles in my throat, and my eyes would water terribly at school. I would run to the bathroom to limit the embarrassment. I think this was my body trying to scream out and let my voice be heard. Once again, I would tell my body to just shut up. I needed to survive somehow.

My father would force us to watch shows and movies with him. He loved seeing our reactions during scary movies. His nervous system did not function the same way as ours, and he rarely showed any signs of reaction. His startle response was extremely minimal, and he did not react to the scary parts of the movies in the same way the rest of us did. We watched Psycho, Rear Window, I Know What You Did Last Summer, and X-Files movies as a family growing up. He loved looking at the sheer terror in my eyes during the terrorizing moments. I existed for his pleasure; I was his literal puppet.

Every humiliating moment was under the guise of constructive criticism. My brother was incredibly bright and scored off the charts in his third-grade standardized testing in math and science. He was fast-tracked for the gifted and talented program that the school implemented the next year. This brought up fears of being "less" in me, and my brother became my rival. I was a great student, but the sleep deprivation during the abuse impacted my school performance. Still, I had to do better to compete for the love and approval of my father.

I was also my father's therapist. When he and Mom were having relationship issues, he would say, "I need you to talk to your mother." This was more about buying a video game system or a new video game. It was typically related to his shopping addiction. He was exempt from the normal day-to-day responsibilities of being in a marriage and the unexpected that comes from being vulnerable with another person. He could not be bothered with the tasks of mere mortals.

My father was a basketball player in high school. He made sure to tell me that he did not play very often and that this was a disappointment to his family. They never came to his games. I picked up on this at a young age, and it was one way for me to connect with my father. He always made sure to find criticism with something I did. I'm sure he rationalized that he was a better parent than they were because he came to the games. The car rides home were always terrifying, and I was sure to be told in extreme detail all of the errors I made. When I said the comments were hurtful, I was told I was "too sensitive" and he was "just trying to help," — an extremely effective gaslighting technique.

I bought Alanis Morisette's CD Jagged Little Pill in seventh grade. Her anger and angst spoke to me during a very troubling time. I was drawn to her song *Perfect:*

Sometimes is never quite enough
If you're flawless, then you'll win my love
Don't forget to win first place
Don't forget to keep that smile on your face
Be a good girl

You've gotta try a little harder

That simply wasn't good enough

To make us proud

I'll live through you

I'll make you what I never was

If you're the best, then maybe so am I

Compared to him compared to her

I'm doing this for your own damn good

You'll make up for what I blew

What's the problem, why are you crying

Around thirteen, I said that I did not want to grow anymore. My dad shamed me for this, of course. At the time, I gaslit myself, but looking back, I think this was my soul's way of longing for a time when I was small, whole, and free from abuse by my grandparents.

When I was starting to develop breasts, my father made sure to body shame me. I remember one day, I wore some pajamas that had shorts and a tan top. My father showed a disgusted glance and told me that it was time to wear a bra. Once again, my body had let me down. My inner critic ran the show by this point. I was stuck in a daily tornado of self-shaming and self-hatred.

I was bullied throughout my entire seventh grade year. One of the boys who "asked me out" in sixth grade, asked me out again in seventh grade. When we spoke on the phone I could hear a click as my father surveilled the conversation. I was not interested in him, so I told him politely no the first time. The second time he asked me out in person, I said yes because I was in my fawn response, wanted to please and feared hurting his feelings. I had no interest in him and after a few days, I broke up with him. Then the floodgates opened. His friends would call me *fat, ugly, hoochie mama* and any other names you could expect. I was harassed most days of the week at school. I'm sure the teachers heard it, but they never intervened. My nervous system would freeze up during these situations based on my conditioning, so I would rarely fight back. I was missing more school than necessary because I was depressed, and my dad shamed me for that. My mom was around less due to her full-time schedule and was engrossed in her trauma, feeling the pressure to pay off my father's insatiable shopping addiction. Neither of my parents knew me well enough to notice that something was wrong. When I finally confided in my mom about the bullying, she expressed sympathy, but no intervention was provided at the school. My dad told me to grow a backbone.

My family was extremely isolated during this time. Neither of my parents had many close friends, and we had limited people over at the house. My toxic shame grew while my worldview shrank. I was expected to feed my brother lunch and clean the house during the summers when we were home with my dad. My mom had some health issues, she was depressed, and there were constant arguments about money. I thought that keeping the house clean would make her happy and keep my family together. I had to survive somehow.

He was the model father whenever friends would come over. He would put on an A+ Oscar performance each time. He would run through the house with the fly swatter if there were bugs in the house. He was especially childlike during these exchanges, living out his inner child that was shamed. When we would all get in the car, he would say "mobilize" which everyone thought was hilarious. He was always the life of the party, and my friends would say, "Your dad is the best!" This led to extreme cognitive dissonance. Clearly, I was the problem, and I just needed to do better.

A close family friend's son died of leukemia at the age of five when I was thirteen. This experience of seeing a child slowly wilt away was heartbreaking to witness. The last time I saw him his skin was yellow, and his cheeks were sunken in. The world seemed so incredibly cruel and dark. During the funeral, I fought back tears as the slide show of pictures played on the big screen. I started to question the existence of God, which only led to more shame.

By thirteen, I was indoctrinated, and feelings were my enemy. One day, when my brother was irritated about something, I shouted, "Stop crying, you're being a baby!" The sheer sight of raw emotion was enough to repel and disturb me. I'm sure my lips curled up in disgust, my toxic shame on display. Every uncomfortable emotion was repressed, trapped in my body.

The Miseducation of Lauryn Hill was my first CD when I turned 14. My father shamed me for this as well because I took an interest in her independent of him. I could escape in my headphones and go to my fantasy world. I knew subconsciously that my soul and life forces were systematically being destroyed.

I wrote these words for everyone, who struggles in their youth

who won't accept deception instead of what is truth

It seems we lose the game before we even start to play

who made these rules, we're so confused, easily lead astray

— Everything is Everything, Lauryn Hill

Another one of my favorites was The Miseducation of Lauryn Hill:

My world it moves so fast today

The past it seems so far away

And life squeezes so tight that I can't breathe

And every time I've tried to be

What someone else thought of me

So caught up, I wasn't able to achieve

But deep in my heart

The answer it was in me

And I made up my mind

To define my own destiny

My father also "confided" in me about some of his childhood trauma and adult grievances. He said that he never felt loved by his father because his parents had to get married when his mother became pregnant with him. His dad did not willingly "choose" to have him, and he felt like a mistake. He did not get braces during childhood, but his other siblings did when the family gained more financial means. His brother picked a college roommate as his best man during his wedding. His sister named my cousin after his brother. His college girlfriend cheated on him with his best friend. He did not have a girlfriend in high school or a date for the prom. He was always the victim, and I was responsible for absorbing his intense pain. This cemented our trauma bond.

During my teenage years, some of my favorite memories were listening to music with my father. He gave me a strong education in classic rock and had a natural inclination toward the deeper meaning of lyrics. When I was about sixteen, we were listening to music in his computer room, and he asked me, "What is this song about?" The name of the song was "Sympathy for the Devil" by The Rolling Stones.

Please allow me to introduce myself

I'm a man of wealth and taste

I've been around for a long, long years

Stole million man's soul and faith

And I was 'round when Jesus Christ

Had his moment of doubt and pain

Made damn sure that Pilate

Washed his hands and sealed his fate

Pleased to meet you

Hope you guess my name

But what's puzzling you

Is the nature of my game

Stuck around St. Petersburg

When I saw it was a time for a change

Killed Tsar and his ministers

Anastasia screamed in vain

I rode a tank

Held a general's rank

When the blitzkrieg raged

And the bodies stank

Pleased to meet you

Hope you guess my name, oh yeah

Ah, what's puzzling you

Is the nature of my game, oh yeah

I watched with glee

While your kings and queens

Fought for ten decades

For the gods they made

I shouted out

Who killed the Kennedys?

When after all

It was you and me

Let me please introduce myself

I'm a man of wealth and taste

And I laid traps for troubadours

Who get killed before they reached Bombay

Pleased to meet you

Hope you guessed my name, oh yeah

But what's puzzling you

Is the nature of my game, oh yeah, get down, baby

Just as every cop is a criminal

And all the sinners saints

As heads is tails

Just call me Lucifer

'Cause I'm in need of some restraint

So, if you meet me

Have some courtesy

Have some sympathy, and some taste

Use all your well-learned politeness

Or I'll lay your soul to waste, mm yeah

Pleased to meet you

Hope you guessed my name, mm yeah

But what's puzzling you

Is the nature of my game, mm mean it, get down

Woo, who

Oh yeah, get on down

Oh yeah

Aah yeah

Tell me baby, what's my name?

Tell me honey, can ya guess my name?

Tell me baby, what's my name?

I tell you one time, you're to blame

What's my name

Tell me, baby, what's my name?

Tell me, sweetie, what's my name?

Taken aback in my fawn response I said that I was not sure.

"This song is about the devil," he said, chills running down my spine when I saw the smirk hit his face.

As I go back and listen to this song, it tells me everything I need to know about him. This slithery stealthiness is his mode of operation. He is not a man of wealth but a man of taste. He has the "best" musical taste, movies, and possessions. He has an air of superiority in all situations. He is smarter and craftier than others. Every true intention must be hidden. Every act of "kindness" is transactional and will need to be cashed in on later. There is no room for authentic love or connection. There is no love for anything, including himself. His soul's purpose in life is to tempt others into sin and destroy their souls.

The day-to-day game is the temptation of sin. My father told me multiple times that his roommate had an altar to the devil in college. I know with certainty that this was not, in fact, his roommate but him. Every day is a game to see how miserable he can make his victims feel about themselves. His game is to ensure the victim identifies with sin and feels shame-based, fatally flawed, and worthless. How could God ever love me if I am so broken? But my father does: "I love you, but nobody else will." When they feel miserable, they are isolated. When they feel isolated, they feel empty — ready to be filled with evil. The devil slowly fills you with the seven deadly sins: pride, greed, lust, envy, gluttony, wrath, and sloth. The seven deadly sins become your entire identity. You are disconnected from your body and spirit, stuck in the prison of your traumatized mind. Your past mistakes replay like a movie in your mind. You are overwhelmed by the aggregate of your life's sin.

Another one of his favorites was *"Behind Blue Eyes"* by The Who:

No one knows what it's like

To be the bad man

To be the sad man

Behind blue eyes

And no one knows what it's like

To be hated

To be fated to telling only lies

But my dreams they aren't as empty

As my conscience seems to be

I have hours, only lonely

My love is vengeance

That's never free

No one knows what it's like

To feel these feelings

Like I do

And I blame you (you, you, you)

No one bites back as hard

On their anger

None of my pain and woe

Can show through

But my dreams they aren't as empty

As my conscience seems to be

I have hours, only lonely

My love is vengeance

That's never free

No one knows what it's like

To be mistreated, to be defeated

Behind blue eyes

And no one knows how to say

That they're sorry and don't worry

I'm not telling lies

But my dreams, they aren't as empty

As my conscience seems to be

I have hours, only lonely

My love is vengeance

That's never free

No one knows what it's like

To be the bad man

To be the sad man

Behind blue eyes

He was upset that Breaking Bad used Limp Bizkit's version of this song at the end. He was noticeably upset about it. His superior taste would have picked The Who version — the original and superior version of the song.

During one family dinner with my mother's parents, we sat down at the dinner table to pray. I closed my eyes and instinctively opened them to check and see if my father had participated in the prayer. His eyes were open in defiance. He put his forefinger to his mouth to shush me about this little secret. Another reminder was that my father was not subject to the rules the rest of us had to follow. And even more sinister, he was evil.

I took guitar lessons in tenth grade. On a subconscious level, I believe this was rooted in deepening my connection to my father. My father said that he played a few instruments — guitar and the flute — but he did not possess a creative spirit. The devil has no room for creativity or authenticity; that is not his game. I eventually started to write music and poetry. I recorded a series of songs with my dad in our basement. My father appeared supportive of this hobby, but he would nitpick something about every song; nothing was ever good enough as I had originally written it. This was a control tactic under the guise of "constructive criticism."

I wrote a series of songs during my junior and senior years of high school. When I went back to listen to the music, I got chills listening to a song about "Adam," a boy I was dating, that was clearly about my relationship with my father:

What can I give to you

That I already have not given

How should I act in public

Just to make you happy

What are the rules tell me now

So I will not break them

I'll always be the one

Always coming back for more

I'll take the blame in the argument

Because it's always my fault

And when you talk of other girls

I'll listen and I won't get jealous

Because I don't know

Of the games that you are playing

And I have trust in you and in us

I have learned that I am worth

More than you'll ever tell me

And I deserve so much better

Than what you're willing to give me

I hope you know you were wrong

In ever passing me by

This is the end forever, so I bid you goodbye

I wrote another song about being sheltered and wanting to become a knowledgeable, worldly woman. The last phrase of the song says, *"The sheltered little girl doesn't always make the wisest woman."* This played into my father's hand perfectly. If I could become worldly, I would be tempted away from God. This would make his manipulation more powerful.

During my senior year, I became very interested in Tool's Lateralus. I listened to the CD relentlessly when I completed my Calculus homework at my desk in my room — the music subtly communicated to me that my achievement in school was my ticket out of this wasteland.

Black then white are all I see in my infancy

Red and yellow then came to be, reaching out to me

Let me see

As below so above and beyond, I imagine

Drawn beyond the lines of reason

Push the envelope, watch it bend

Over thinking, over analyzing separates the body from the mind

Withering my intuition, missing opportunities and I must

Feed my will to feel my moment, drawing way outside the lines.

I was obsessed with Vertical Horizon's Everything You Want. I learned how to play this song in my senior year, and I would replay it over and over. Listening to it now at thirty-nine, the song is less than stellar, but the lyrics tell the story of a girl who was dying for validation from her father:

I am everything you want

I am everything you need

I am everything inside of you

That you wish you could be

I say all the right things

At exactly the right time

But I mean nothing to you and I don't know why

And I don't know why

His mask came off when he lost control. My first boyfriend did not meet his impossible standards. He was a year older and dropped out of high school. He was not very intelligent, and he did not challenge me intellectually. But he gave me something I longed for and did not get from my father: love that was not transactional. He made it clear to our extended family and anyone else who would listen that Brandon was a moron. During my high school graduation party, we were very affectionate, and he later told me it was very embarrassing for him. His rage was kept neatly tucked away until there was no audience. I did not execute my part flawlessly, and he made sure I knew it.

One argument when I was seventeen escalated dramatically. I was asserting my independence, and he was close enough to my face that his venomous saliva hit me. I remember my whole body trembling after leaving the house — confused because I was not physically harmed. Why does my body keep betraying me?

I overdosed on Advil shortly before turning eighteen. I was tied up in some drama with Adam, and instead of receiving support from my friends, they told me I was being too sensitive. My father told me that "life wasn't fair" to his glee. I told my mother immediately, and she took me to the emergency room. She said, "I would go to hell and back for you," as they pumped my stomach. I think subconsciously she knew we were already there.

Part II: Adulthood Before Motherhood — 19-34 Years

"[11] 'For I know the plans I have for you,' declares the Lord, 'plans to prosper you and not to harm you, plans to give you hope and a future. [12]Then you will call on me and come and pray to me, and I will listen to you. [13]You will seek me and find me when you seek me with all your heart. [14]I will be found by you,' declares the Lord, 'and will bring you back from captivity.'"

— Jeremiah 29: 11-14, NIV

At eighteen, I left for Albion College. The school was about two hours away, and I relished the freedom. The school had a Methodist background, which was similar to my Presbyterian upbringing. I could set my class schedule, take the classes I wanted, wake up when I pleased, go to bed whenever I wanted, and eat what I liked. I had a roommate who was a huge pothead and drinker. I had been indoctrinated against drugs and alcohol, so I stayed away from them during my first semester, playing the "good girl" part. I remained with my boyfriend during the first semester, but I quickly realized that we were growing apart. I broke up with him during Christmas break of my freshman year.

During that break, I spent a considerable amount of time with my best friend from high school, Krystin. She had gotten a job right after graduation and did not attend college. There was a guy at her work named Sean, who was a few years older, and we would hang out with him, going to the local bar to play billiards. After I broke up with my boyfriend the day after Christmas, I reached out to Sean to hang out. I was lonely and wanted to get out of the house. It was late, around 10 p.m. or so. My father had provoked me that day, and beneath all the trauma, I knew on a subconscious level that the house was not safe. I had a curfew and was concerned about my dad freaking out, but Sean said he would pick me up in my neighborhood, and we'd go back to his place to watch a movie.

When he picked me up, I noticed he had been drinking. The drive back to his apartment was about twenty minutes. When we got there, we started messing around, and eventually, he tried to initiate sex. I told him I wasn't interested. My boyfriend had been the man I lost my virginity to, and I only wanted to have sex with someone I was committed to. He pressured me relentlessly. Even through my tears, he continued until I eventually relented, dissociating and going into my "fawn" trauma response. The pattern was well ingrained in me — to play dead to avoid being "eaten." By the time he brought me back to my house, it was around 1:30 a.m. It was December 27th — my 19th birthday.

When I got home, I felt numb. My body was full of unprocessed energy, and I found it difficult to sleep. Mid-morning, I collapsed in my mother's bed. I spoke to no one in my family about what had happened. Looking back, I was itching to be taken care of, but too afraid to ask.

My second semester of college became a period of self-exploration. I started smoking marijuana with my roommate and other close friends, taking drives through the country at night. I began skipping class more often, lost interest in studying Spanish, and started drinking alcohol. I attended fraternity parties and started dating one of my roommate's friends who lived in Charlevoix, about three hours from school.

That summer was filled with pleasant memories. I got a part-time job at Sears in the Lawn and Garden department. My boyfriend and I would alternate weekends at each other's places. We spent a lot of time smoking marijuana, taking nature walks, listening to music, watching artsy movies, talking about our views of the world, and discovering ourselves. I also lost about thirty pounds during the summer.

I received a movie education that summer. We watched *American Beauty*, *The Devil's Advocate*, *The Matrix*, *O Brother, Where Art Thou?*, and *A Beautiful Mind*, among others. I started to notice parallels between the antagonists and my father. My father was incredibly manipulative, but he had a very soothing voice meant to instill a sense of calm obedience. In any argument, he would say, "to play devil's advocate," which, in retrospect, was very telling. I related deeply to Neo's dilemma between the red pill and the blue pill — the painful experience of choosing to see the world for what it really is versus the blissful ignorance of going through life without the clarity that opens you up to hurt and betrayal. Growing up, my father forced me to watch scary and disturbing movies with him for his entertainment. Picking the movies I watched became my way of taking control of my narrative and worldview.

During my sophomore year of college, I started attracting a lot more attention from men. My skin was incredibly tan from all the time spent outside during the summer. I was thin and toned from exercise. As a person struggling with toxic shame, my identity was wrapped up in how other people perceived me. My mood, self-worth, and perceptions were all tied to how others viewed me. I started running in the evenings after classes. My favorite CD during that time was Radiohead's *OK Computer*. Running was my time to escape the ruminating thoughts in my head and dissociate. The physical movement made me feel like flying away from my problems was possible. For those thirty minutes, I was free — not a prisoner to my own self-doubt and harsh inner critic. I thought I could outrun my past and even God's influence in my life.

That year, I was exposed to an excellent English literature teacher. Ms. Jordan's class changed my life. I loved escaping into prior time periods and stories. Literature was the perfect mix of history and art. My need for knowledge was insatiable, and my goal was to become a worldly woman. I also enjoyed analyzing writing for themes, reading context, and developing arguments to support my points. My childhood had primed me for distinguishing the world of nuance.

My abandonment fears kicked in, and I decided to transfer to a local college in the second semester of my sophomore year to maintain my relationship with my boyfriend. I felt open about my opinions with him, but I was extremely disconnected from my feelings. My standard answer when he asked how I was feeling was, "I'm fine," but my body language and facial expressions often suggested otherwise. I had difficulty making simple decisions, like what type of food I wanted for dinner or what I wanted to do. The simplest choices seemed like monumental tasks to me and drained my mental energy.

I got an apartment on campus and visited my maternal grandparents during the week for dinner. I was incredibly lonely and escaped into the world of my studies. Academia was a world with clear rules — one in which I could excel.

During this time, I learned about a concept called the "numinous," which was life-changing for my spiritual life. Writers during the Gothic period wrote about the divine and supernatural power of nature, a quality I had always felt. Shakespeare's *Hamlet* underscores this during an exchange between Hamlet and Horatio. Hamlet says, "There are more things in heaven and earth, Horatio, than are dreamt of in your philosophy." Hamlet says this to Horatio after Horatio describes a confrontation with his father's ghost as "wondrous strange." There are some experiences in life that simply transcend logic and typical understanding.

Later that year, I declared English as my major in college. The study of the human experience was both fascinating and healing for me. I read *Incidents in the Life of a Slave Girl*, *Beloved*, *Frankenstein*, *Jane Eyre*, *The Waste Land*, *The Awakening*, *The Sound and the Fury*, *Pride and Prejudice*, and *The Great Gatsby*. I connected deeply with the stories of longing and loss. I was drawn to tales of self-actualization. On a subconscious level, I knew my authentic self was at war with my childhood persona. Slowly, I walked out of survival mode. Step by step, I found my voice.

I moved back to my parents' home during my junior year. My father guilted me about the cost of the apartment, saying that my parents couldn't afford it. This was an obvious control move, and I fell for it, holding on to hope for a truly authentic relationship with a man who created an incredible amount of cognitive dissonance — holding two contradictory beliefs at the same time. On one level, my father was present and provided some degree of parental guidance. On another level, he was manipulative, degrading, and self-righteous.

As a dutiful daughter, I enjoyed the company of my mother and brother. At twenty-one, my brother was seventeen and a junior in high school. We became close, connecting over music — the language of our family. I relished the fact that my brother deeply valued my boyfriend's opinion.

I had forgiven you for tricking me again

But I have been tricked again,

Into forgiving you,

What is this? Are you some kind of hypnotist?

Waving your powers around - the sun eclipse behind the cloud

I thought I recognized your face

Amongst all of those strangers,

But I am the stranger now

— Are you a Hypnotist, The Flaming Lips

In my senior year of college, I had a small distraction. I would frequent the local bars on the weekends when I didn't see my boyfriend, and I met someone who needed my help. He was a tall, 6'3" red-haired man with a victim story. Charismatic and charming, he showered me with attention and compliments. I was transfixed.

One day, he got caught for stealing a CD at Walmart and called me from jail, asking me to bail him out. I "loaned" him $100 for bail, which I never got back. He also lost his job at Burger King, claiming his co-workers were conspiring against him. My boyfriend and his family were exasperated when I decided to drive four hours to his grandmother's home in Indiana to get a vehicle for him, which he said was the key to his independence.

However, after arriving at his grandmother's house, I was given some excuse as to why the vehicle wasn't ready. We left a few days later, empty-handed.

My friends Jason and Alisha had also interacted with him. They told me that he was a narcissist. They had allowed him to stay at their place as a goodwill gesture since he was without a job. Jason said that he had been speaking to other girls and was a pathological liar. He was lazy, unconcerned about how his behavior impacted others, and never offered to help with any bills. After a few weeks, he was kicked out of their place.

This news was surprising to me. How had I missed the signs? Why was I drawn to helping this person when I had little financial means of my own as a college student? Why would I risk my relationship with my boyfriend to help this "lost puppy"? I internalized the shame of this experience and severed all ties with him.

I would catch glimpses of my father periodically in the basement at night when we crossed paths. Whenever I caught him off guard, I was terrified. His piercing blue eyes lacked depth or humanity. It was as if he had no soul. I would jump back in shock, thinking my reaction was due to the unexpected meeting. But it went deeper than that. My body remembered, and it was reacting. His stare was predatory.

During college, I struggled with the concept of God. I questioned everything I had been taught as a child. I had learned about inequality, subjugation, and the pervasive force of evil in the world. When I was around ten years old, I began questioning the seemingly ridiculous rules and laws of the Old Testament, such as keeping the Sabbath holy and not performing any work on that day. How do we define "work"? Isn't breathing work? Isn't eating work? What about the role of women in the Bible? Could I be a strong woman and still be a Christian?

One of the most transformative classes I took in college was on Shakespeare. *Hamlet* reminded me of my father. The play was about an uncle trying to take Hamlet's place as the heir to the throne using deceptive tactics. One of my professors mentioned that *The Lion King* was based on *Hamlet*, and that made sense to me. I had loved the Disney movie, which came out in 1994, just before my tenth birthday.

Shakespeare often used women as key figures in his plays. In *A Midsummer Night's Dream*, the night represented the unconscious desires of men. The fairies were villainized as temptresses, responsible for men's unwanted or unsavory desires. The feminine spiritual energy was powerful and, thus, had to be repressed. Rosalind is a key figure in Shakespeare's *As You Like It* and is known for her beauty, quick wit, and resilience. One of her famous lines is "I pray you do not fall in love with me, For I am falser than vows made in wine. Forever and a day. O, how bitter a thing it is to look into happiness through another man's eyes!"

The Tempest was Shakespeare's last play. In it, he explores his role as the creator of his own plays, essentially playing God. This is a role reserved for those with creativity and spiritual energy. The play also deals with themes of subjugation, with "othering" being a key element. By "othering" people, you could degrade them and create a case for domination — whether through slavery, psychological brainwashing, or other means. Slowly, I realized that this had been my childhood experience.

I wrote a poem titled "The Wall" about a man who shamed me sexually. At first, I thought the poem was about him, but I eventually realized it was really about my father.

He is a man with leg like bricks

Tall and stiff

This poem was published in a book when I was twenty-two. I had completely forgotten about it until this year. I asked my mother if she could find the book so I could refer to the full poem, which escapes my memory. She couldn't find the book anywhere. I'm sure my father threw it away.

After I graduated from college, I broke up with my boyfriend. He lacked motivation and was growing marijuana in his apartment. While we connected intellectually, I wasn't attracted to him. He didn't fit in with my high school friends, and I didn't see a future with him. As a worldly, educated woman, I felt I needed a successful man by my side to gain the approval and acceptance I so deeply longed for.

I also took up running. There was a park full of pine trees and sandy dirt about five minutes from the Lake Michigan coast that I would frequent. I would lose myself in the music and the rhythm of my feet hitting the soft earth. I was getting that familiar itch again — I needed to take flight.

I was working at my mother's place of employment in a manufacturing role after multiple college internships. It was unfulfilling work, but it paid the bills. I sent my resume to various creative outlets — copywriting, editing, etc. — but got nowhere. I felt extremely stifled, living under the judgmental environment of my youth, with my parents' watchful eyes scrutinizing every decision I made. I remember my uncle stating, "What do you do with a BA in English?" as though it was a useless degree. That was very hurtful.

That fall, after college graduation, I visited South Carolina with my friend Alisha. During the trip, I met Justin while we were out together, and I continued to speak with him after the trip. I started applying for jobs and eventually received an offer for a call center position. I made plans to end my lease early and accepted the job offer. I loved the thought of a fresh start — an opportunity to create my own future, away from the control and influence of my parents.

At work, I looked up to a co-worker, Dave, as a father figure. He was a Quality Engineer, interested in music, art, and politics. He was intelligent and witty, and we had a very similar sense of humor. He was in his mid-forties, married with two children, while I was twenty-two. I was seeking companionship and the selfless love that a good father provides. I thought our relationship was platonic, but he made sure to tell me that he was in love with me, which made me feel visibly sick.

When I was twenty-two, I had an unsettling experience one night while in the hot tub. I saw my father peer through the blinds in the darkness, letting me know he was watching me. He had a habit of walking by just as I was wearing my bathing suit, sizing me up like a predator. It was a very unsettling feeling and had the air of control, rather than that of a protective father.

My gift of self is raped

My privacy is raked

And yet I find, and yet I find

Repeating in my head

If I can't be my own

I'd feel better dead

— Alice in Chains "Nutshell"

One of my coworkers was a huge Alice in Chains fan. I fell in love with the angsty lyrics and dramatic tones of *Nutshell*. There was no space to find myself while living so close to my parents; their influence was overwhelming. My community was small enough that I would regularly run into high school friends. I needed to find myself, and I needed to do it on my own terms.

I slowly came to the realization that my father was extremely dangerous. I broke my lease, sold my furniture, bought a new vehicle, and moved twelve hours away. My mother and I drove together to South Carolina, and she flew back afterward. My sweet mother supported me in my decision to grow.

I packed my Mazda Protégé 5, and my mom and I embarked on the twelve-hour drive to South Carolina. My flight instinct kicked in, and like Tinkerbell, I flew away. We listened to Outkast and John Mayer, and we admired the beautiful mountainous scenery — God's creation — with possibilities at my fingertips. It's interesting to reflect on this now; twelve is the number of order, government, and perfection in the Bible.

As much as I tried, I couldn't run away from my past. Not surprisingly, I was drawn to the familiar pattern from childhood, and my boyfriend Justin mirrored my father in many ways. The love-bombing stage was incredibly intoxicating. I was told how beautiful I was, sent romantic songs and poems — the perfect cocktail for my creative spirit. Once reality set in, my feelings were invalidated. I was made to feel insecure about my physical appearance, my body, my intellect — all components of myself. He shamed me for not keeping the apartment clean enough. I drank too much when I was with his friends and embarrassed him. I took his biting sense of humor too seriously, and I was "too sensitive." Yet, through the pain, there was a strange comfort in the familiar dynamic.

I met my roommate Angela at my call center job. She was incredibly empathetic, funny, and an English major in college. I enjoyed talking with her about our love of books. We were both feminists, and I valued her worldview. I confided in her that I was struggling with my faith, especially with reconciling the overwhelming evil in the world. She recommended C.S. Lewis' *Mere Christianity* to me, which would change the course of my life.

C.S. Lewis' *Mere Christianity* completely shifted my worldview and understanding of God. He argues that humans are guided by a law of human nature about right and wrong that is innate, but we routinely fall short. The existence of evil, he explains, is goodness spoiled and used for evil purposes through the gift of free will. One of my favorite lines from the book is: "If a thing is free to be good it is also free to be bad. And free will is what has made evil possible. Why, then, did God give them free will? Because free will, though it makes evil possible, is also the only thing that makes possible any love or goodness or joy worth having" (pages 47-48). Lewis further argues about the danger of Satan's independence from God: "What Satan put into the heads of our remote ancestors was the idea that they could 'be like gods' — could set up on their own as if they had created themselves — be their own masters — invent some sort of happiness for themselves outside God, apart from God. And out of that hopeless attempt has come nearly all that we call human history — money, poverty, ambition, war, prostitution, classes, empires, slavery — the long terrible story of man trying to find something other than God which will make him happy" (pages 48-49).

Eventually, I decided I'd had enough of the verbal abuse and severed ties with Justin. He had a college degree, worked in sales at Enterprise, and decided to go back to school for an engineering degree. The coursework and time commitment created distance in our relationship. He lived on campus with students seven years younger than him — young men in a different phase of life. He asked if we could share a vehicle. I was trying to get my career off the ground and was tired of being belittled by someone without a job. I was tired of taking care of everyone else.

When I broke up with Justin, I called my father. He picked up immediately, as he always did. I was the family member he kept under the tightest surveillance because I was the one who could "out" him as his true self, well hidden behind the mask. I told him that I feared him. He was 6'5" and had never been physically abusive, but he was very emotionally abusive. Every social interaction was criticized. I always committed some social inadequacy. My clothing was either too provocative or not provocative enough. I was either too kind or not kind enough, too friendly or not friendly enough. The list went on.

I felt intense fear of him and told my father. He asked, "Why were you scared?" I explained that it was because he was so angry and a foot taller than me. I was replaying my childhood in my adult relationships. I had an inkling that this might be at play, but I don't think I fully realized it at the time.

I was young, single, pretty, and ready to party. I attracted toxic people because I was full of toxic shame. I went out to bars, drank too much, and made poor choices. I spent too many nights in the company of men. I woke up regretting my decisions, embodying the toxic shame that had been thrust upon me in childhood. I was a beautiful contradiction — I believed that being submissive was my path to love, based on my childhood patterns, while also holding the fierce spirit of "this little light of mine" in my back pocket. My spirit and soul were at war with one another.

I started a job in human resources at a large corporation. I was young, pretty, and intelligent. I attracted a lot of attention — from both men and women. I interacted frequently with the operations team during interviews and disciplinary processes. One of the production managers, Sean, took an interest in me. He was 6'4", handsome, charismatic — the usual cocktail. He love-bombed me harder than anyone ever had. He even placed a picture of himself on my phone receiver, which cracked me up. He called me "gorgeous" and "sugar lips." I was showered with gifts, dinners, love notes, compliments — you name it. The dopamine rush was overwhelming.

Our relationship was toxic. We were young and good-looking, and I thought that shallow love without depth could persevere. We spent a lot of time at his grandparents' house on the lake, drinking all weekend. By the time we got back to his place, our emotions would get the best of us. We went to church the next day as repentance for our love of all things worldly. We both fixated on the idealized version of our relationship, terrified of the dark parts of our own souls and of each other.

I had a pregnancy scare early in the relationship. I told him my period was late while we were in the fruit aisle at the grocery store. He told me, "If you're pregnant, I'll throw you down a flight of stairs." It was a "joke," but my doctorate in nuance sensed a deeper meaning. I was subservient in this relationship, and it was best for me to realize this early on. My basic survival needs of food, shelter, and belonging were met, so it made sense for me to stay in the relationship. I had minimal friendships or external influences, as I had recently moved from out of state. I was the perfect target for emotional abuse.

Sean proposed within a year of our relationship. He proposed on April Fool's Day, which led to confusion among family members. Looking back, this was a definite red flag. I was twenty-six years old.

By that time, I had internalized the "cool girl" image — the "go-with-the-flow" girl who has no needs. Self-deprecating humor was my armor against the world. I was terrified to cry. Three adult relationships and an unhealthy childhood had left me with no template for determining whether someone was the right fit for me. I didn't even truly know myself. My autonomy had been devalued my entire life. I had no experience having hard conversations about values or goals with a partner. I was not allowed to argue as a child. My job was to willingly submit to my father's rules.

My father chose Tom Petty's "Wildflowers" for our father-daughter dance during my first wedding. It became one of my favorite songs because it captured my ethereal, free spirit perfectly.

You belong among the wildflowers

You belong in a boat out at sea

Sail away, kill off the hours

You belong somewhere you feel free

Run away, find you a lover

Go away somewhere all bright and new

I have seen no other

Who compares with you

When I listened to the song again at thirty-nine, I sobbed uncontrollably. The realization hit me that he knew all along I was connected to the spiritual realm. He knew my essence, but it was more important for him to stifle me because that meant I could be controlled, manipulated, and used. This realization was me swallowing the hard-to-swallow red pill.

It's not surprising that this marriage was doomed to fail. As Jimi Hendrix said, "And so castles made of sand fall into the sea, eventually," in his song *Castles Made of Sand*. I decided I wanted to have children, and my husband joked that if I got pregnant, he would shove me down the stairs. I also married a bigot — his sister was gay, and his family was very openly against her "choice." Her own mother said she thought she was going to hell. This did not align with my values or my view of what it means to be a Christian. My Christian mantra is Jesus' commandment in Mark 12:29-31:

"29 'The most important one,' answered Jesus, 'is this: 'Hear, O Israel: The Lord our God, the Lord is one. 30Love the Lord your God with all your heart and with all your soul and with all your mind and with all your strength.' 31The second is this: 'Love your neighbor as yourself. There is no commandment greater than these.'"

I secretly found an apartment and moved out less than two years into our marriage. I still remember him leaving while I was packing my things, coming back late at night, and doing donuts in the backyard — a childish game to show his disdain for me asserting my independence and freedom.

It's not my job to judge people. That is God's job. My job is to love people and show them God through the Holy Spirit that lives in me. Everyone is fighting a battle, and making assumptions about what others are going through keeps us from offering them the kindness we are asked to give as Christians.

"I'll be fine on my own, " she said.

"I don't need you inside my head."

(She'll be fine on her own, she'll be fine on her own)

"I'll be fine on my own, " she said.

"All my love's wrapped in shades of red."

(She'll be fine on her own, she'll be fine on her own)

Growing pains, splaying rain on the high sea

Scale a tree, snap a branch, so you can't leave

On the ground, lost and found, understand me

Putting words in my mouth, trying to get free.

— Hippocampus Buttercup

The year 2014 was the darkest year of my entire life. I couldn't run away from my thoughts, job, or relationship. I was living in a one-bedroom apartment in a loud neighborhood and unsafe area. I was going through a divorce, a clear failure of everything that had been prescribed to me as a child of the church. I lost my job when the company I worked for transitioned its manufacturing plant overseas. I also had a procedure performed to remove pre-cancerous cells from my uterus. I was twenty-nine, childless, without a job, house, or husband. My perfectionist façade, based on achievement, came crashing down. My main sense of comfort during this time was my chiweenie, Chloe — the one relationship in my life where I felt loved unconditionally. She also provided a sense of comfort and safety. I was in deep survival mode, stuck in my own psychological prison.

I went to my childhood home for Christmas in 2014, expecting to be welcomed with kind and loving arms. Instead, my parents were so heavily involved in my brother's issues that they had no space for my needs. To be fair, my brother was deep in trauma and loss, but I felt incredibly neglected. If anything, I was probably looked at as the savior of everyone, the parent of each individual in my family. I started smoking to help regulate my nervous system, a habit I picked up from my husband. My father shamed me for this. It was a reminder that I was not perfect, which led to further toxic shame.

I started reading self-help books to help me understand what went wrong in my marriage. I knew my father was emotionally unavailable, and I did not have the idealized relationship or a fierce protector full of adoration. I developed a list of traits that were must-haves in a partner, mostly based on values. On the "must-have" list, I included someone who believed in God, was kind, reliable, interested in sports, and desired to have children. I realized that charisma was a blind spot of mine, and I wanted actions to guide the relationship. Words are meaningless without actions behind them. I needed to do the uncomfortable homework upfront before falling in love again. I needed to be practical this time around.

I went to church and listened to praise music relentlessly. I broke down crying during services. I was completely and utterly broken and helpless. I prayed for God to bring me a man who would be my perfect complement and with whom I could start a family. At thirty-two, I was still childless, and I wanted to be a mother more than anything.

One of my best friends during this time had narcissistic tendencies. She stepped over any boundaries I set and was always the victim in every situation. She knew I wanted to have children and told me that she wasn't sure we could be friends once I had kids because it would cut into her time with me. Her childhood was traumatic, but she refused to get professional help. Her coping mechanism for everyday stress was to drink or escape into the problems of others. My father met her and said she had narcissistic tendencies. He was the expert; he would know.

I dated online relentlessly, using Match.com, Plenty of Fish, OkCupid, Bumble, and Tinder. I had as many terrible experiences as I did positive ones. Some men expected my body in return for dinner, which I found degrading and disappointing. But I also found decent men who were searching for a life partner. It was because of this daring pursuit that I met my husband, Matt.

I eventually met my second husband, Matt. He was kind, compassionate, a sports fanatic, religious, and wanted children. We had in-depth conversations about our goals. He was more emotional than my prior type — he was a Cancer. I was incredibly repressed in my feelings and logical at this point in my life, and I sometimes got uncomfortable during deep conversations. But he never shied away from tough discussions. We married after two and a half years of dating, and I became pregnant with my son, Lucas, on our honeymoon.

I was hesitant about the typical wedding festivities. At the time, I thought this was a control move, but looking back, I think it had more to do with my social anxiety and fear of public humiliation. My husband and I initially wanted to have a destination wedding, but we were guilted and persuaded into having a more traditional wedding by our family members. During my father-daughter dance, my dad's performance was extremely over the top and cheesy, to the point where I stopped the music early. He was humiliating me to make a point. He couldn't handle that I was in the spotlight, and instead of directly communicating, he chose to passive-aggressively mock a sacred moment.

On the drive up to the ceremony for my second wedding, I was extremely stressed. I had to wake up at 6 a.m. for hair and makeup to be done for the 11 a.m. ceremony. It was an hour-and-a-half drive to the wedding chapel. My dad joked, "Is this going to be your final wedding?" laughing hysterically at my unease as my brother talked about the latest Kanye West album. I was near a panic attack as I changed into my wedding dress. Walking down the aisle, I visibly sighed. I was in survival mode, terrified of the public humiliation I feared would come on a day that was supposed to be special for me. I knew subconsciously that my father didn't love me and was terrified of what he would do.

We got married outdoors at "Pretty Place" in South Carolina, an outdoor chapel and an extraordinarily spiritual place. The Biblical verse "I will lift up my eyes to the hills" (Psalm 121:1) is posted at the top of the chapel, with a cross laid out directly in front of our ceremony. I cried before I recited our vows, and we kissed before we were pronounced husband and wife. After a life of public humiliation, I had developed terrible social anxiety. I put aside the stress of my father's words and tried to enjoy the moment. At our reception, we had a wood hanging that read, "I have found the one whom my soul loves." — Song of Solomon 3:4. It hangs in our master bedroom to this day.

Part III: Motherhood — 35-Present

"For we are God's handiwork, created in Christ Jesus to do good works, which God prepared in advance for us to do."

— Ephesians 2:10

Words and names possess special meaning to me. It was only natural that my son's name be rooted in scripture. My son's name is Lucas. The Latin name literally means "bringer of light" and comes from the verb *lucere*, which means "to shine." Luke is the third book in the four Gospels. Luke is a physician, and the name in Greek means "one who heals." This is incredibly fitting, as Lucas' birth started me on my healing journey.

Labor with Lucas was incredibly painful and arduous. I was induced at thirty-nine weeks due to my age. I was in labor for about twenty hours. My hips were uneven, and I had difficulty progressing past five centimeters dilated. My doctor said a C-section was becoming imminent. I was vehemently against this. I had to be perfect and succumb to my penance of childbirth. I was in active labor with him for about forty minutes. At one point, I had four nurses over me and a tie bar. I kept saying, "I can't do this!" But I had love and support surrounding me, and I persevered.

Lucas' birth healed me in many ways. I will never forget the awe I felt at my first glimpse of him. As John states: "A woman giving birth to a child has pain because her time has come; but when her baby is born, she forgets the anguish because of her joy that a child is born into the world" (John 16:21). Lucas clarified many things in my life. I cared less about comparing myself to others. I was less jealous and more loving. I had more empathy. I was more emotional, kinder, and slowly became more patient.

Motherhood was still a difficult transition for me. It was hard for me to move between my mother persona and my work persona. Going through pregnancy and the newborn period during COVID was extremely stressful and isolating. We received an extremely demanding project at work that year, requiring a lot of extra time and effort. I was not sleeping well, waking up in the middle of the night thinking about all the tasks that were left undone. Looking back, I could feel my perfectionist mask cracking. I couldn't keep up the act, and I felt like an imposter.

I became pregnant with my daughter Ava shortly after Lucas turned one. Ava is a variation of Eve, coming from the Hebrew name *Havva*, which means "life" or "lively." My husband and I agreed to try for another child; I always wanted two children, and I was blessed to have one of each sex. I received a significant promotion when I was seven months pregnant. Fortunately, I was able to take twelve weeks of paid leave after giving birth. I wanted a boy and a girl, with the oldest child a son who could look after his sister and offer her protection. Like all things, this had a deeper meaning for me that makes perfect sense now.

During my pregnancy with Ava, one of my best friends, Jadie, passed away. She died at the age of forty-one from colon cancer. The news was devastating. I got physically sick after her passing. She was one of the few people who truly knew me on a deep level and made me feel seen, felt, and heard. We shared a love of God, and we talked extensively about the Holy Spirit's presence in our lives and how it spoke to us. I took her passing as a reminder that our time on earth is short and that we need to make it count. I also made my health a priority.

I couldn't wait to return from maternity leave. The to-do lists at home were dwindling, and I was terrified of being alone with my own thoughts. I was deep in survival mode. My brain was not functioning to its optimal capacity — I noticed that I had to read sentences of books numerous times to comprehend the content. I had difficulty maintaining my attention. I spaced out regularly. I jumped headfirst into work. My job required more travel than I was used to. My mom guilt was strong whenever I was away from my kids. I felt like I was always letting either my family or my co-workers down. I was always disappointing someone, and this brought my deep childhood trauma wounds out of the shadows.

I was very emotionally reactive. My work environment was full of triggers: direct emails from co-workers, not meeting the expectations of authority figures at work, a leader of the business who resembled my father, Ava falling behind in her first-year milestones, the deteriorating cleanliness of my home, the revolving shopping list of clothes, shoes, and diapers for the kids, and the weight of carrying the bulk of the family's financial burden. The responsibilities were overwhelming, and I was drowning. There was no way I could be perfect in these conditions. My inner critic controlled my day-to-day life with reckless abandon.

I knew myself well enough to realize I needed help. I reached out to a therapist. The issues I wanted to work through were my transition into motherhood and the resentment I felt toward my husband. I found a psychotherapist with strong somatic training. We started with a chronology of my childhood. We talked about the birth of my brother and the death of my grandmother when I was four. I completely downplayed the severity of the issues. She also noted the traumatic car accident I was in when I was eight, the bullying I faced in seventh grade, and the rape I endured at nineteen. I was incredibly disconnected from my feelings, running on autopilot.

One conversation stood out to me. We were talking about a situation where I was bullied in seventh grade, and I told her that my response was to "fawn," essentially playing dead. She asked, "Where do you think that came from?" That led me to believe that this pattern was already ingrained at that point. I thought back on all the comments my father made to me throughout the years, the resentment and contempt sprinkled into each one, and I started to realize that my father was the original bully.

One of the key focuses during our sessions was on developing a sense of safety. I was regularly asked, "How does that make you feel?" and I felt completely disconnected from my body. As we went through my history, I talked about my previous interest in playing guitar and writing music.

"Why do you think you stopped playing guitar?" she asked.

"I'm not sure. I lost interest," I said.

My therapist noted that my right hemisphere and frontal lobes were offline. I was functioning without over half of my brain. I became extremely frustrated when we transitioned to visualization exercises because my subconscious was a black void. I dissociated regularly and found it difficult to be present in my body.

Fitter happier

More productive

Comfortable

Not drinking too much

Regular exercise at the gym (3 days a week)

Getting on better with your associate employee contemporaries

At ease

Eating well (no more microwave dinners and saturated fats)

A patient, better driver

A safer car (baby smiling in back seat)

Sleeping well (no bad dreams)

No paranoia

Careful to all animals (never washing spiders down the plughole)

Keep in contact with old friends (enjoy a drink now and then)

Will frequently check credit at (moral) bank (hole in the wall)

Favours for favor's

Fond but not in love

— "Fitter Happier" Radiohead

At thirty-eight, I had achieved more than I ever realistically expected, but I still felt empty. I provided a comfortable living for myself and my family. I obtained a job that I had dreamed of, at a salary I never expected. I had a beautiful home, two beautiful children, and a loving husband. Yet, I was terrified of having a moment of open space while also being emotionally and physically exhausted. I filled every spare moment with tasks, chores, TV shows, and podcasts. Silence was terrifying to me. I would do anything to avoid being alone with my own thoughts.

What was missing? Why wasn't my dad proud of me?

My childhood wounds started to play out in my work life. I was constantly on edge at work, waiting for something terrible to happen. A direct email from a co-worker was perceived as an attack. I was constantly in defense mode, feeling the need to justify every decision I made. I became highly irritated when people who worked for me did not follow my instructions.

"Why are people so stupid? Why can't they get it right?" I thought.

I was the highest-ranking woman in my company, and I felt a sense of responsibility to be an example for other women. I was surrounded by men who were close to my father's age, with a similar build and demeanor.

An incredibly triggering situation at work occurred. One of the site leaders was transitioning into a new role and was required to keep the information confidential until receiving approval from the corporate office. This person did not keep that promise and claimed that someone locally had been told by me about the change.

I lost it on a call and said, "She's lying!"

I was told by a senior leader to settle down and was shamed for having a natural reaction to being accused of something untrue. I confirmed with the local source that this conversation had never happened. The senior leader said to just brush this under the rug; my job was to silently absorb this blow without a word, like I had done my whole life.

No sir, I was done being silent.

Emancipate yourselves from mental slavery

None but ourselves can free our minds

— Bob Marley, Redemption Song

I slowly started to take my narrative back, step by step. I confronted the co-worker who made the inaccurate comment about me. He apologized and said that it was all a "misunderstanding." His response meant less to me than the feeling of empowerment I felt in standing up for myself, asserting my human right to dignity and respect.

I took on the habit of running. This appealed to my flight response; there were times when I literally felt like I was flying away, running away from my authenticity. I ran a half marathon during the fall and passed out about 0.25 miles away from the finish line. I had no memory of falling. 911 called my husband, and I could not answer what day it was or what year it was. My work family was texting me, concerned that I was not at the finish line. I did not have the cognitive capacity to make a phone call. I was rushed to the emergency room in an ambulance. My first thought was about suicide, albeit very briefly.

"Why couldn't I just finish the race? Why does my body keep letting me down? Why can't I just be perfect?"

For Christmas that year, my parents stayed at my house. I started doing yoga and somatic body work at the urging of my therapist, and I felt extremely charged when my parents were there, finding it difficult to get to sleep. I also read the book *The Body Keeps the Score*, which highlights how stored memories and emotions are held in the body as pain. My father made constant comments about the house:

"You should get blinds in this room instead of curtains. Your garage is messy; should we take some of the old boxes to the dump? The lighting in this room is off. Your dog is not house trained yet. When are you going to move back to Michigan? I just drove twelve hours. I want to be able to enjoy our trip; can we go out to dinner? Ava is getting quite chubby."

The "constructive criticisms" were endless and reminded me of the narrative I had eventually internalized, which was adept at pointing out all the ways that I was deficient. I confronted my father and told him that the constant nitpicking whittled away at my self-esteem. He seemed unfazed by the comments and said that he "loved me very much" and he was "just trying to be helpful." The comments felt flat and insincere.

My world turned upside down when my son ran into some trouble at daycare at the age of three. The owner of the school was emailing daily about issues with his behavior. We started therapy for my son once a week. The situation escalated to a crescendo when he was suspended for four days one week for hitting a girl in his class. This was not appropriate behavior by any means, and it was not my proudest mom moment. But the abandonment wound hit deep. I had to keep it all together with work meetings, watch my child for four days, and go to a bachelorette party for my sister-in-law Lauren at the end of the week while keeping the "good girl" smile on my face the whole time.

After coming back from the bachelorette party weekend, I toured a new school for my son. I instantly connected with the teacher, a mother of a two-year-old child with special needs. I got emotional as I explained the issues that Lucas was facing. Lucas transitioned to the new school within a week.

It took me a while to process the experience and understand why this was so traumatizing for me. Lucas was within a year of the age that I was when my brother was born and my grandfather passed. I was simultaneously taking care of my son and nurturing my inner child that had felt abandoned. I was reparenting myself with the love and care I never received as a child.

I could not avoid seeing myself in Ava. When I rocked her prior to placing her in her crib, I felt like I was rocking myself, giving myself the love and affection I had so desperately longed for as a child. I saw the body shaming from my father already starting for her at one year old. I witnessed the love and care her grumpa showed her when she lay in his arms at our aunt and uncle's pool, reminding me of the feeling of complete safety I had felt in my grandfather's arms at his lake house. His adoration for her reminded me of the adoration I had felt from my grandfather. Her obsession with her "dada" reminded me of my obsession with my father.

A few months later, my sister-in-law's wedding day came. I took Friday off work to prepare for the wedding and rehearsal dinner. I got a massage and a pedicure, prepped the kids' clothes, and cleaned the house before the 3:30 PM rehearsal dinner. When I dropped the kids off at daycare that morning, I told the owner that I was picking them up mid-afternoon, and she suggested picking them up at 1:45 PM to avoid nap interruptions.

At 12:50, we received a text message from my mother-in-law:

"Are you home? Kids are dying to see Luke?"

Husband: "I am picking the kids up at 1:30."

Mother-in-law: "Why?"

Husband: "Because I just got home from work and don't want to disturb nap time at daycare. On our way, and both were sleeping, so I had to wake them up."

Husband (2:02 PM): "Home."

Mother-in-law: "Not coming. Too late. We have to leave here by 3."

I lost it. I took a day off work. My entire day was focused on wedding preparation and activities. We rushed to get the kids early, only to receive the rude response that we were too late. We had an entire hour before the kids needed to leave for the rehearsal dinner for them to play with their cousins. The response was very hurtful and hit my perfectionism like a ton of bricks. The kids would be seeing their cousins the entire evening. Why was nothing ever good enough? Why couldn't we get it right? Why couldn't we just be perfect?

The rehearsal dinner was at the venue where my husband and I got married. My sister-in-law, Liana, made rude comments when I was trying to connect with my nephews about racing to the door.

"Way to go, Liz! You're going to get them all riled up!"

I was in survival mode the whole evening. I could not regulate my nervous system by taking deep breaths. I was not present during conversations. I drank an excess of white wine that night, falling asleep in the car on the way home.

The day of the wedding brought my trifecta of social anxiety, harsh inner critic, and perfectionist issues to the surface. I sweat through my bridesmaid's dress during the ceremony and was told by my husband's uncle that I received the reward for "best cleavage." All my body shaming from childhood came back, and I was extremely self-conscious throughout the day. I dissociated during pictures and was reminded that I was not following instructions, which only multiplied my shame. My husband's stepmom, Brenda, said,

"Get it together, Liz!"

It was a teasing comment in retrospect, but it brought my harsh inner critic front and center. I saw the example of what a father's love looks like on his daughter's wedding day: the kiss on the cheek or forehead, the tears, the utter joy and adoration. All the feelings that I subconsciously questioned but was afraid to know the answer to. And lastly, my son, at three years old, decided to ham it up while walking down the aisle and talking during the ceremony while I was up in front of the stage "performing." My mask broke. Everyone was looking at me, and I felt like I was ruining the ceremony. There would be hell to pay.

Not surprisingly, people thought that my son's entrance was funny, and it was the high point of the ceremony. Lauren and her husband could not hear my son during the ceremony, and he did not distract from their special moment. I was not humiliated for being an incompetent and terrible mother. But I was still mentally and physically exhausted by the time 9:30 PM hit at the reception. I brought the kids home while my husband enjoyed the festivities with his family late into the evening.

When I left with the kids, my husband's father kissed me on the forehead, saying,

"You looked so beautiful,"

a pure gesture of love and kindness that I will never forget and was more affection than I ever received from my own father.

I took a sabbatical from therapy and started Belleruth Naparstek's "Healing Trauma" Guided Meditation on YouTube. I was feeling stuck, and my therapist had a subtle attitude that came across as shaming, which felt like a light electric shock to my heart. The exercise was about sixty minutes and was broken up into two parts: one part guided imagery and one part affirmations. My body trembled excessively during the guided imagery part. I slowly started to visualize different aspects of the exercise. I sobbed during portions.

One evening, I woke up in the middle of the night, and my entire right arm trembled and shook for thirty minutes. My range of motion increased in this area of my body, and I remembered that my right arm was the part of my body that was outside of the jeep during my traumatic crash at eight years old when the car toppled over. I noticed much less muscle tension between my shoulder blades. This also fulfilled my Christian duty of seeking God in secret wholeheartedly.

"⁴Tremble and do not sin; when you are on your beds, search your hearts and be silent."

— Psalm 4:4

I also regained a series of memories from my childhood during these exercises. I remembered my grandparents' house on Lake Michigan in exquisite detail. I could feel the cold, wet sand between my toes, the seagulls softly squawking in the background, the refreshing breeze, the cleansing water, and the brilliant colors of the sunset. There was the feeling of utter safety and comfort as I sat in my grandfather's arms in a wooden chair. This was my oldest home, the part of me that could never be destroyed.

I continued with the practice daily; it became my soul's nourishment for the day. I was rushed with a series of repressed memories from my childhood. I could see each room of my childhood home in detail, and I was flooded with feelings that were stored in my body. My gut area would tremble as my intuition slowly came back online. My body shook as it gradually released the stored trauma that had been hidden for so long. The subject of meditation is covered numerous times in the Bible; my favorite verse is Psalms 19:14:

"May these words of my mouth and this meditation of my heart be pleasing in your sight, Lord, my Rock and my Redeemer."

One afternoon, I had an epiphany during this exercise. I felt my whole body vibrating during the affirmations portion and felt a literal blanket around me during the "I feel a warm blanket of comfort surrounding me." I sobbed uncontrollably at the last sentence of the practice:

"I know I am held in the hands of God, and I am perfectly, utterly safe."

I felt complete, like my mind, body, and spirit were all online and slowly guiding me back to my authentic self. There was a sense of calm within my spirit that day, awakened after a long sleep.

I reached another breakthrough the following week during the exercise. My children's school was closed due to a water leak, and I was working from home. I found it impossible to be "perfect" during this time, but I held my own on a series of work calls, muting myself on Microsoft Teams when Lucas or Ava would cry in the background. I put the kids down for a nap around noon and went through my guided meditation, interrupted by my husband, who left work midday to support me. I was flooded with a series of thoughts and truths that needed to be uttered.

I told my husband about how difficult my childhood was. I felt the weight of the world on me as a young child. I shared that I felt the need to parent everyone and that so many expectations were placed on me. I knew my mother was depressed and unhappy, so I always tried to cheer her up. I was my father's therapist and wife, subject to the day-to-day chores, cooking, and cleaning. My mother was too traumatized to parent my brother, so I tried to take on that role. I also felt like I was not allowed to have needs growing up; they were not advantageous to my survival and were repressed. It was incredibly difficult for me to express my needs, to the point of being painful. When I said I needed something, I needed him to know that I really needed it. My feelings of resentment toward him for not sharing the responsibilities of parenthood stemmed from my unmet childhood needs of having to take care of everyone else while not having the space to be taken care of. It was the ultimate moment of vulnerability, and it felt so incredibly freeing.

I also reached out to my parents about my memories. I called my father one Sunday afternoon while he was on his walk with my mother and asked if he remembered my uncontrollable sobbing at my grandfather's funeral. He said that he did not remember this. He was noticeably irritated with me during the conversation, which was odd. My body remembered incredible pain during this time, so I most likely stored the pain but did not have the words or body reactions to express the trauma in a healthy manner at four years old. I left the conversation feeling uneasy, as if my father was purposely withholding information from me.

The following week, I talked to my parents about my memories of my grandfather during our weekly portal video session with the kids on Sunday morning. My father asked me to call him afterward to have a one-on-one conversation. I told him that I remembered feeling dearly loved by my grandfather, and he downplayed this, saying,

"I guess he loved you,"

and that he became very sick with brain cancer when I was about two years old, so we had a limited relationship. I told him that my memory said otherwise. He mentioned that his father was incredibly rude to him when he was sick during an exchange where he was called an "asshole" for having to use the bathroom when he held up scheduled plans.

"I was not talking about you; I was talking about my experience," I said.

Instead of validating my experience, he gaslit me, saying,

"Are you sure this repressed memory thing is healthy for you?"

It seemed like manipulation to me. I talked through some of my past traumas with him, and my father downplayed this, saying that if anyone had PTSD, it was my brother, given his history of trauma. I left the conversation feeling incredibly charged and upset.

That afternoon, I told Matt,

"I think my father is a narcissist."

My body was trembling during the entire phone conversation, my alarm system signaling that something was not right. He agreed immediately and told me that he knew this the first time he met my father back in 2017.

"Why didn't you say anything?" I asked.

"Because he's your father," was his response.

I cannot think of a moment when I felt more loved. He did not want to ruin the illusion I desperately grasped of the sacred relationship between a father and daughter. Furthermore, he was willing to subject himself to that person for the rest of his life with a woman he loved.

My father's narcissism did not manifest in the typical grandiose fashion. I started doing some online research and learned that there was a form of narcissism called "covert narcissism." These individuals were typically more introverted and always played the victim in any circumstance. Check. As I continued my research, I learned that covert narcissists disguise their criticism of you as helpful advice. Whatever you think of doing that connects with your authenticity leads them to ask, "Are you sure you want to do that?" When you communicate your feelings to them, they twist it as, "I'm only trying to help you," a subtle sabotage that they present as advice and helpfulness.

One of the books I purchased was *The Covert Passive Aggressive Narcissist: Recognizing the Traits and Finding Healing After Hiding* by Debbie Mirza. The book states that covert narcissists will constantly criticize and judge you in undercover ways that are not always obvious. This enables them to control you as your self-worth slowly declines. Your sense of value erodes over time. You see yourself as being unlovable, not wanted, and too much or not enough.

I had a feeling of immense validation during one passage of this book:

"The 'golden child' is lavished on and treated with more kindness. This can seem like a nice thing for this child, but in fact, it puts them in the position of trying to be perfect in order to keep that love and attention. They watch as their siblings are treated differently. They naturally want to keep that good feeling of being loved by their mom or dad, so they learn early on how they must behave to be treated with love. This sets them up for a life that is filled with the pressure of never being less than perfect in anything they do. It has been instilled in them that this is how they get people to love them and keep their love and attention. They also don't expect to be unconditionally loved, so often they choose partners who don't treat them with consistent, pure love. They never feel good enough and can live with underlying despair and unhappiness for a long time." (page 94)

Later that week, I went to my friend Michelle's house. I told her and her girlfriend, Stacey, about my realization regarding my father. My whole body trembled on and off for about three hours as I was flooded with memories and realizations. My friends were extremely alarmed and worried about me, but I told them that it was healing to release the tension and that I was doing so because I felt safe with them. My intuition provided me with the information that I needed to go no contact with my father. I was flooded with memories of watching television as a family during my childhood, with my father forcing me to watch programs with him for his entertainment as he talked about how attractive all of the girls and women were, knowing that it would speak to my jealousy and my devilish side. I remember covering myself with a blanket to hide my trembling body. I did not want him to see the effect he had on me. It was also telling me that I needed to cancel the trip I had scheduled to Michigan with Lucas a few weeks ahead of us. My childhood home was not safe.

There was one video from Meadow DeVor on YouTube titled "5 Clues to Spot a Covert Narcissist in Conversation" that was incredibly uplifting. She talked about an overwhelming tendency for them to fish for sympathy. The dialogue orbits around their misfortunes, which is a way of hooking you to support their needs. They want pity but argue against any reasonable solution. I remember multiple conversations where I told my parents that they should seek therapy. My father was less interested in a solution and more interested in soliciting my pity.

Covert narcissists use passive-aggressive comments disguised as casual remarks. They will drop subtle digs about friends, colleagues, or you. When my parents were at the house during the spring holiday this year, my father said, "You really need to get the puppy potty trained because you don't want to have to buy new carpet," which seems like a relatively harmless comment to an outsider, but he was doing this to subtly degrade me and let me know that he did not approve of Rex, my mini bernedoodle's potty training. When my parents would stay at the house, I was told, "You need a bigger TV for watching football games," or "You should get blinds in place of curtains." I purchased a new bed for my father to sleep on when he stayed at our house. My husband and I carried the mattress upstairs on Christmas Day. My father was upset about the futon we had for them to sleep on, and I went to Ashley Furniture the day after coming home from the hospital after Ava's birth to buy a new couch for him. The saleswoman there was appalled that my father was asking me to do such a thing after my body had been through such a difficult event. My father set up a gaming computer in our spare room and later told me I no longer needed it after a few years, expecting me to pay $850 for a computer I did not want. He mentioned that I could change the password, and I blew it off at the time.

The third trap is the savior's trap bait. It is a manipulative technique to make you feel needed. During one trip to Michigan, my father told me, "You may need to support your mother and me financially" when my parents became older because my brother was still living at home and draining their financial resources. He told me this during a one-on-one conversation at the dog park, where we were the only people around. I left the conversation with a sense of responsibility and pity. I had moved out of the home and had been living on my own for years, but his influence on me was evident.

Contradictory valuation and devaluation is a fourth sign. After a promotion at work, when I talked about how much I valued my relationship with my boss, Jeremy, my father said, "Don't sleep with your boss." What kind of father says that to his daughter? The shame I felt with this comment cannot be understated. How could my father make such a demeaning comment to me after a huge accomplishment that I had made?

The fifth sign is a subtle sensitivity to criticism. During my parents' trip in the spring of 2024, my father made it clear that he would like to do some activities outside of the home for fun. I scheduled time at the play center downtown Greenville. My father complained about the traffic, the number of people that were there, and the setup of the place. The happiness and joy of his grandchildren were of little value. I called him out on this, saying that he was negative and acting like a toddler. He retreated to his bedroom, and I felt the need to comfort him. He took no accountability for his responsibility in the exchange.

Michelle Lee Nieves Coaching on YouTube has a video titled "The Traumatized Personality of Victims of Covert Narcissistic Abuse." Her therapist said that the imprint of narcissistic abuse is very distinct, clear, and obvious. She states that we utilize our midbrain 24/7. This portion of our brain is needed for life-and-death situations and is the least evolved part of our brain. Narcissistic abuse ignites our fight-or-flight trauma state. When we are not in our prefrontal cortex, we cannot see joy, grasp the big picture, or make clear decisions. When we are stuck in our midbrain, our fear response is overactivated; we do not have access to our memory, our brain struggles with rumination and highly intrusive thoughts, and we remain in a place of fear. When this happens for an extended period, we develop the five symptoms of complex PTSD: self-abandonment, toxic shame, a harsh inner critic, social anxiety, and emotional flashbacks. Our entire identity becomes our trauma response. My primary trauma response is flight. My constant activity turned me into a human doing rather than a human being.

Dr. Ramani, considered an expert on narcissism, has a video titled "How to Think About Your Narcissistic Parent" on YouTube that was very impactful for me. The video is broken down into 11 steps of advice:

1. "You were robbed." A narcissistic parent is a special kind of hell: decades of day-to-day meanness, pettiness, invalidation, manipulation, and gaslighting. I was robbed throughout my childhood of validation, of a parent who sees me and who can put my needs first.
2. Acceptance is a temporary solution. I felt this one deep. I constantly vacillate between acceptance, depression, and anger in the grieving process, sometimes within hours of each other. I will be comforted by the fact that I have answers, only to find myself depressed a few minutes later because my father never showed me the love or care that my boss showed his

daughter when he bought her first car and was giddy with excitement for the sheer joy she would feel when she found the car in her driveway. I'm full of rage because I spent so much of my life feeling like I was the problem and that I needed to be "better" to be worthy of love. Unconditional love does not need to be earned; it is given willingly. But I operated under the assumption that it could be won by my actions. If I could just get it right next time, maybe I would get the approval I was so desperately seeking. I was filled with rage to know that the withholding of love was a deliberate tactic by my father, used to keep me grappling for the affection that he would intentionally never show.

3. Stop gaslighting yourself. I tend to downplay the severity of the abuse because it is incredibly difficult to come to terms with it. It has a profound impact on my worldview to realize that a key relationship in my life was all a lie — a complete fabrication.

4. This was not your fault. I needed to hear this. I spent so much of my life feeling like I deserved my father's treatment because of who I was. I internalized the thought that there was something inherently wrong with me and that I was not worthy of love. The only way I could "win" love was to become more perfect and devote my life to tireless self-improvement.

5. Stop saying that your parents sacrificed so much. My father provided a home and shelter for me. I had clothes to wear, and he came to my basketball games. My expectations of him are so incredibly low. Continuing to rationalize his treatment is not healthy for me and will disrupt my healing. To heal, I needed to stop downplaying the severity of the abuse.

6. You may not be at peace with your parents until they pass. I had a conversation with my husband, expressing that I would feel more at peace with myself once my father passed away and was no longer able to abuse anyone. I felt immediate guilt after this statement, but it was my truth that I wanted to live.

7. Step away from enablers and prune your family tree. When I came to the realization that my father was a narcissist, I told my mother. She was initially in the bargaining phase, asking if I could set boundaries rather than keep him from my children. During the phone conversation, she said, "It seems like you are angry." I replied, "I am angry. I told you that I did not feel like my father loved me, and you did not see me or hear me during those moments. You told me that Dad loved me in his own way. Your son also told you that Dad was a narcissist, and you did not see or hear him."

8. With the grey rock method, there is no right answer. The "grey rock" method is a tactic to be as uninteresting as possible to the narcissist so they move on to another source of supply. I am struggling with these options right now. I blocked my father on my phone, but he and my mother are still texting my husband. They left a message for one of my friends the other day. I had to cancel a trip home with my son for my own mental health. After I made up a COVID excuse not to travel, I told my mother that I needed a break from the group text for my mental health.

9. Stop excusing the narcissistic parent based on their backstory. This one hit me hard. I made excuses for my father my entire life because of all the injustices done to him: a father who did not love him, a cold mother, a girlfriend who cheated on him with his best friend in college. The list goes on.

10. Stop getting stuck in the "if it had only been different" vortex. The allure of self-pity was very intoxicating. I spent time ruminating about who I would be if I had a supportive and loving father. Would I have a different job? Would I live somewhere else? My upbringing had some benefits, including my incredible independence, my strong work ethic, and my endless empathy for others. There was a lot to be grateful for. Next, she recommends reparenting yourself. She talks about healthy parenting behaviors: unconditional love, safety,

mirroring emotions, supporting and encouraging aspirations, compromising, and self-sacrifice. I have already been doing some work here. During my flashbacks to particularly difficult memories, I imagined myself coming in to save my child self, removing her from the situation while telling her that she was safe and that this was not her fault. These exercises were incredibly powerful and helped me develop the self-compassion that I had missed.

11. Your parent will never change. I found some odd solace here. It was comforting knowing that the person who seemed to be so incredibly unpredictable was going to follow a relatively predictable pattern. He could not be "saved," and it was not my responsibility.

In my research, I stumbled upon a video titled "Strange Behaviors of Narcissistic Abuse Survivors." The hair on my arms stood up in validation. All of these behaviors described me perfectly:

Hypervigilance: I was in a constant state of fight or flight, scanning my environment for threats. I felt incredibly on edge in cars with males and experienced a sense of unease on airplanes when I had to sit next to other people, particularly males. I had incredible difficulty relaxing. I regularly took shallow breaths, particularly when under stress. I lived with a low-level fear that something terrible was about to happen.

People-Pleasing Tendencies: I have a habit of trying to manage everyone else's emotions. When someone is upset, it is physically painful for me, and I believe it is my responsibility to make them feel better. I make a habit of checking in on my friends, particularly when I know they are going through a difficult time. I find it physically painful to tell someone no, and when I do, I feel the need to justify my decision in exhaustive detail. I do this to seek the approval that I so desperately needed during childhood.

Self-Isolation: My bedroom has always been my escape. During my childhood, I would lie on the carpet right next to my CD player while the music helped me regulate my emotions. I would sit in my butterfly chair and get lost in a book. In adulthood, I retreat to my bedroom after I put my children to bed each night, turning out the lights to minimize stimulation, losing myself in a book or TV show on my iPad. I feel like an electronic device depleted of battery that needs to be recharged. When I become irritable and impatient, I know it's time for me to step away from human interactions and regain energy in solitude. I find it much easier to process my emotions privately rather than discussing them with others. I found scripture to support this:

"⁶But when you pray, go into your room, close the door and pray to your Father, who is unseen. Then your Father, who sees what is done in secret, will reward you."

— Matthew 6:6

Apologizing Excessively: I feel responsible for items completely out of my control. I apologize if the weather is bad. I apologize for the traffic when we are driving. I apologize at work when candidates do not show up for an interview. I feel responsible for every wrongdoing. I have noticed this behavior in myself and try to police it more so I do not jump to immediately apologizing if I am not responsible. It's a work in progress.

Difficulty Making Decisions: I get frustrated with making dinner choices; if I am particularly hungry, I will tell my husband to pick. I can be indecisive at work and will ask team members for their recommendations. The self-awareness of this difficulty has been managed lately by stepping away from the situation for more complex decisions and revisiting it when I have the mental capacity to evaluate with a fresh mind.

Obsessing Over Personal Relationships: I ruminate over conversations both in person and via email or text ad nauseam. I spend more time after the exchange trying to decode some hidden meaning. This stems from my father's subtle changes in facial expression, tone, or body language that alerted me to threats. I had to be a detective of these nuances as a coping mechanism to ensure my survival. The first step is recognizing when I do this and trying to switch to another action to change my thought pattern.

At the end of the video, the author talks about two gifts that emerge because of narcissistic abuse: resilience and empathy. I escaped from my hell of a childhood, started my life over, created my own path in a rewarding career, met the love of my life, and created a family. I am fiercely independent and capable. I have rewarding relationships with people who truly love me for my authentic self. I am hyper-aware of other people's feelings and can tune into them with surgical precision. I choose to be kind and empathic to people. It is a choice   God's greatest gift to us is free will. I know how it feels to be deeply unseen and unheard, so I try to listen to others. I lift other people up with kind words or gestures. I enjoy giving back to others in need. I try to be there for the ones I love when they need me.

I started sending my mother and brother a wealth of content about covert narcissism. My mother was shocked at the accuracy of it. The evening after I sent out a series of videos, my brother came into my mother's room at 2 AM, trembling, independent of my text messages. He told her that my father was sending threatening text messages and that he was a narcissist and an evil person. It was the most validating moment of my entire life.

My mother reached out to a narcissistic abuse recovery line and was matched with a therapist who focuses on narcissistic relationships. I had a conversation with my mother and brother on the phone. I had not spoken with my brother since my wedding in 2019, a period of about five years. My brother had been trying to tell my mother that my father was a narcissist for the past year. He had told her multiple times, and each time she dismissed it because his narcissism was not present in the typical way.

My father is incredibly adept at realizing what people's insecurities are and exploiting them to his benefit. My mother's shame was her management of my brother's situation. My father would constantly tell her that she was enabling him, which is a complete projection. My brother's family role was the scapegoat. My father blamed him for everything wrong with our family. My father had to externalize his shame to remain perfect. This, of course, could be no further from the truth. My father was full of flaws. My brother was one vessel of shame;

there was limited space for anything else. Somehow, he still found space for God. He told me, "God bless you," during my wedding to Matt, which touched me deeply. His empathic spirit was still dimly lit inside.

My father had some subtle hints for his game. The computer monitor in our spare room was the Predator brand. My father would always tell me, "Watch out for predators," whenever I would run. He could get away with this because it could be interpreted as the words of a caring father. But I had cracked the code: this was a clever way of portraying a loving father while also subtly instilling fear in me.

The age of eight was a pivotal year for me. I was in third grade, and it was the same year as our tragic car accident. I rewatched the Chronicles of Narnia, C.S. Lewis's masterpiece. My teacher read this book during my third-grade year. I was taken aback by a few things. The "fawn" in the tale was too timid to set boundaries or stand up to the evil witch, the physical representation of Satan. This classifies my mother perfectly. She knows my father's true essence on some level, but she is terrified to block his evil deeds. The other piece that stood out was the fact that Edmund, one of the children, did not enter the same reality as everyone else. His entire reality was sin; he had no space for God. His siblings were trying to save him, but they were told that only Aslan, the representation of Jesus, could save him. It's not our job to save others; only God can do that. We can, however, listen to our brothers and sisters in Christ (our family) about their visions of God. If they are in Christ, their visions have meaning and need to be heard.

That same day at church, the sermon talked about the different needs between men and women. We talked through the controversial passage from Paul in Ephesians 5:22-23:

"²²Wives, submit yourselves to your own husbands as you do to the Lord. ²³For the husband is the head of the wife as Christ is the head of the church, his body, of which he is the Savior."

Our pastor said that women have a need to submit to their husbands, but only if the husband meets the different levels of love. There are four different types of love: Eros — romantic, sexual passion; Philia — affectionate regard through friendship; Storge — affection between parents and children; and Agape — unconditional love, the love of Christ. Women are only required to submit to their husbands if they show their wives Agape, the unconditional love of Christ. He said that men will not get a woman's body until they get her heart. The pastor stated that this did not apply to women outside of marriage; many women are successful businesswomen, entrepreneurs, and political figures, and their voices are valued in their professions. The pastor also said that all people are welcome in the church and that the church does not belong to a political party.

I sobbed quietly at the validation. All I ever wanted was to be loved unconditionally. I did not need someone to take care of me financially, buy me endless gifts, love-bomb me with intermittent reinforcement, or treat me like a child. I needed love that mirrored the love of Jesus. I knew that the sermon was the word of God, and I felt a deep sense of safety in being seen.

That same evening, I had an Eye Movement Desensitization and Reprocessing (EMDR) session with my psychotherapist. This method involves moving your eyes left to right to activate both the left and right hemispheres of your brain while you process traumatic memories. EMDR's goal is to help you heal from trauma or other distressing life experiences. I told her that I had a lot of charged energy about the laundry room in the basement of my childhood home. I was flooded with several memories about being in the basement during the summer between second and third grade. I slept in the basement that summer because we were putting an addition on the house, and our third bedroom was being converted into a master bathroom and bedroom. My mother confirmed that my father was sleeping in the basement that same summer because he snored so loudly that he kept her up.

I knew that I had been violated in some way. EMDR uses bilateral stimulation — tapping of the left and right hand — to activate both hemispheres of the brain. She first asked me to picture an incredibly soothing place. I told her that this was the beach on Lake Michigan from my childhood. I could feel the cool sand between my toes, hear the soothing crash of the waves, feel the soft cool breeze, smell the salt in the air, and hear the seagulls flying overhead.

She then asked me to call in two protectors. I picked Jesus and Aslan, the lion from C.S. Lewis' The Chronicles of Narnia. She asked me to pick two wise figures; I picked C.S. Lewis and my great-aunt Ginny. She then asked me to pick two healers; I picked my close friend Kimberly and my trainer and close friend Tiffany. I would tap left and right until I felt the essence of each person. This practice was done to establish a sense of safety to activate the subconscious.

We then moved to the room where she asked me on a scale of 1-10 how charged the situation felt. I said it was a 6. I could picture the wooden slats on the doors leading in; I was eight years old. The wooden cabinets, washer and dryer, mattress, and hangers surrounded me. I told her that I had a lot of tension in my left hip and chest area. She told me to tap left and right and report what feelings or emotions came up.

I closed my eyes and immediately felt my left arm shaking uncontrollably. I had an incredible amount of tension in my left hand to the point where I could not lift it equally with my right; I was left-handed. My left hand started convulsing, and I knew that my father had asked me to give him a hand job. My arm was convulsing terribly because he did this as he did not want me to make an account of what he did. If I could feel shame in my left hand, it would silence my voice; my God-given spirit was beautiful — more precious for Satan to steal.

I know that my father made me perform fellatio on him. I came up gasping for air, ridding myself of all his toxic energy. He would play Madonna's song "Like a Prayer" for me; there is a line that says, "I'm down on my knees, I wanna take you there." He would push me on my knees and force me to do unspeakable things to silence my voice; he used a secular song against me purposely.

She told me to continue going with that feeling, and at first Aslan scratched him while Jesus picked me up and took me up the stairs. We shut the door to the basement.

My therapist said, "Good! Keep him in his dungeon!" (The basement of a home is typically associated with someone's unconscious mind.) She asked what I wanted to tell him.

I said, "My body is a temple! I am fearfully and wonderfully made! This is your shame! I am wiped clean!"

"2Rather, we have renounced secret and shameful ways; we do not use deception, nor do we distort the word of God. On the contrary, by setting forth the truth plainly we commend ourselves to everyone's conscience in the sight of God."

— 2 Corinthians 4:2

She asked me to go back to the laundry room and tell her how charged the feeling was on a scale of 1 to 10. I said it was a 2. I went back, and Aslan scratched him; I kicked, punched, and hit him. Then Jesus turned him into a mouse, and Aslan ate him.

She asked, "What do you want to say?" I replied, "I am precious. People love me for my authentic self. I am so dearly loved," as I sobbed. I told her I would go out to the tree in the backyard, climb one of the branches, and look at the red, green, and yellow leaves. I wanted to feel the wind blowing and the soft sunlight, a reminder that God was with me. I affirmed, "I never had an earthly father, but I have a spiritual father." She told me to be soft and gentle with myself after the session because we had opened a portal. She suggested that I drink warm tea to soothe myself.

I slept terribly that evening. I was terrified and flooded with traumatic memories. My father abused me at night, so this was a triggering time. I remembered praying to God when I was being abused that He would take me to heaven when I heard my father's footsteps outside my bedroom door. I made sure that Rex was in bed with me and would hear any intruders. Matt has a habit of falling asleep on the couch, but he tried to come into the bedroom before falling asleep. I put on praise music in the morning to help center myself. I got myself ready, got my kids ready, packed their lunches, and put on my multi-step makeup routine. I did all my regular grounding techniques. When I got to work, I realized that I had left my laptop at home.

The old Liz would spend four hours shaming herself for why she couldn't be perfect: "You're so stupid. You're such an idiot. How could you forget this?" But not the fearfully and wonderfully made me who had shed her toxic shame like dead skin. This Liz is allowed to make mistakes. She is allowed to have zits, a muffin top, hair out of place, or chapped lips. Her value is self-evident and sacred. It is not determined by what she looks like that day. It is not determined by how many glasses of wine she had the night before. It is not determined by how many ounces of water she drank. It is not determined by how many calories she ate that day, or what time she started to eat, or how many meals she had. Her value is self-evident and sacred — a gift that only God can give.

One of my work friends, Melissa, had tea waiting for me in my office the following day. I sobbed when I saw the small bag on my desk.

I knew God was looking out for me and leading me down this path. I also knew that He would not give me more than I could handle.

I slept on and off that evening. I woke up in the middle of the night with frequent nightmares and memories. I felt multiple pains in my left hip and between my shoulder blades. I was tormented by my memories, secretly asking God, "Why do they torment me? This is too painful; I want to get out of this hell." It was so terrifying. Finally, in the middle of the night, as I put on my praise music, I was able to self-regulate my nervous system.

I am what is called a Super Empath. Rebecca Zung, on her YouTube channel, talks about the special powers of people with these abilities. Narcissists are afraid of losing their supply; they are more afraid of you than you are of them. They are jealous of you because of the fact that you feel. They hate that you can connect with people. Narcissists vibrate at a level that is well below the authentic level of the super empath. Narcissists have no identity; they feel that other people are always making them mad and are the source of their rage. People who are truly in their power are at peace and are caring. Those who attract a narcissist have a core wound or self-love deficit. This fits my mother perfectly. This type of person feels that helping the narcissist will fix the core wound within themselves. The more healed you become from your trauma, the less and less you can coexist with a narcissist. That is kryptonite to a narcissist.

"I'm living if you can if you could call it living."

— Bambi by Hippocampus

Narcissists are drawn to empaths, and they suck the energy out of them like a vampire. But instead of drinking your blood, they drink your soul, soaking in it like a child basking in the sun. The witch in *Malevolent* lures the child in with a delicious apple, tempting her into sin. The younger the child, the bigger the fall. Jesus said in Matthew 19:14: "Let the little children come to me, and do not hinder them, for the kingdom of heaven belongs to such as these."

My healing was fast-tracked by a new fascination of Lucas's. He was obsessed with the big bad wolf. This perked up my mama bear ears. The wolf is used throughout nursery rhymes to represent someone's cunning intent disguised as helpfulness. Did my father abuse him? I talked to Lucas about this one morning, and thankfully, he confirmed that my father did not touch him anywhere off-limits. He was never alone with my children, so luckily, I was in the clear.

I continued to be flooded with memories that were trapped in my body. I remembered that when I was being abused, I would "hypnotize" my father. I would tell him, "You are getting very, very sleepy," and I would serve as his therapist. During this time, he would express his unconscious desires to me via psychological terms, such as Carl Jung's "shadow," which denotes someone's unconscious. My father would take this time to talk to me about the ways in which my authentic self was "bad." He would say that my shadow was responsible for any sin I committed. In reality, anything that I was blamed for was his unconscious sin. But to deflect blame or guilt for it, he had to project all of this shame onto me. A young, impressionable child is the perfect target. As long as I remained stuck in shame, I was caught up in my sin and could not connect to my authentic purpose. Breaking through your toxic shame is an essential component of connecting with your life's purpose, ordained by God.

The Bible talks about shamelessness:

"27Your adulteries and lustful neighing, your shameless prostitution! I have seen your detestable acts on the hills and in the fields. Woe to you, Jerusalem! How long will you be unclean?"

— Jeremiah 13:27

My father knew that Bruce Springsteen was my favorite artist when I was very young. "Bruce Mic" was one of my first words, which translates to "Bruce Music." I loved music from the very beginning of my life. My father played "Secret Garden," which talks about a little girl's secret garden and that he is the only person who could access it. I felt evil for "tempting" him with my feminine body. Evil Eve was responsible for tempting Adam away from God, and I was responsible for paying the price of subjugation.

She'll lead you down the path

There'll be tenderness in the air

She'll let you come just far enough

So you know she's really there

Then she'll look at you and smile

And her eyes'll say

She's got a secret garden

Where everything you want

Where everything you need

Will always stay

A million miles away

— Secret Garden Bruce Springstein

My father knew I was gifted intellectually and used it against me. He would also play Bruce Springstein's "Brilliant Disguise" whenever I was involved in a worldly activity that is part of a child's normal development. My normal childhood curiosity was seen as a threat to his power. This chastisement of course meant that I was not perfect:

[Verse 2]

I heard somebody call your name from underneath our willow

I saw something tucked in shame underneath your pillow

Well, I've tried so hard, baby, but I just can't see

What a woman like you is doing with me

[Chorus 2]

So tell me who I see

When I look in your eyes

Is that you, baby

Or just a brilliant disguise?

Shaming a woman for her body is a way to keep her psychologically imprisoned. If she cannot connect with her body, she cannot work through her trauma and determine her higher, God-ordained purpose in life.

God is perfect; the world is evil.

Through this turmoil, God looked at me and said, "Dear one, I know you are hurting, and I know my promise to you." I had to regularly dissociate and leave my body to reach the spiritual realm, but this left my body full of pain and unprocessed trauma.

"Dear sister, if you are in terrible pain, God is looking at you, saying: 'For I know the plans I have for you,' declares the Lord, 'plans to prosper you and not to harm you, plans to give you hope and a future.'"

— Jeremiah 29:11

If He can save me from my utter depravity of sin and shame, you can also be saved. He loves you enough to see you through the pain if you maintain faith.

I know inherently that all my writings from high school and college have been destroyed by my father. All of my "gifts" from him, which were laptops, were secretly being surveilled by him. My father destroyed all my writing intentionally because he wanted to destroy my spirit. My spirit exists in my subconscious. It is all there; it is sacred and cannot be taken away by anyone but me through my own willful action.

My job became more and more unmanageable. My heart was tender, and I was very easily triggered. The trauma release exercises were key to my healing; my body would tremble uncontrollably in my bed at night as memories, visualizations, and emotions would come up gradually after safety was established.

It turns out this is noted in the Bible:

*"[9]Worship the LORD in the splendor of his holiness; **tremble** before him, all the earth."*

— Psalm 96:9

As my trauma was slowly released, my right brain came online. My creativity returned, and my range of motion significantly improved. I could dance freely without pain. My hips gradually released trauma, and my hip pain while running — a motion where I brought my right leg in a roundabout motion rather than straight ahead — was significantly improved. My posture was more upright and regal.

Instead of looking down at my shame, I looked straight ahead at all the beauty in front of me each day. There were people all around in my day-to-day activities who wanted to connect with me and could be shown the love of God. Nature served as a reminder of God's beautiful creation. I took the time to listen to the birds, admire beautiful flowers, and watch the clouds gliding beautifully across the sky. There were a multitude of small reminders each day that God was with me and looking out for me.

We had a few changes on the horizon at work. One of our core businesses was up for sale. The chances of a sale were imminent, and a lot of extra work was required to present to potential buyers. My closest human resources work friend, Mara, was the Director of Human Resources for this business unit. I also had another close friend, Melissa, who was going to be leaving the company. During one of our yoga sessions, I had a panic attack when our fitness instructor, Tiffany, said her typical, "I bow my heart to all of you ladies, namaste." Melissa and Tiffany cradled me like a child, telling me to take deep breaths as I calmed myself down. I had met incredible people who became my work family, and the inevitability of it being ripped apart brought my abandonment trauma front and center.

When I was a teenager, I was obsessed with *The Exorcist*. The subject of being possessed by Satan fascinated me, and I wanted to understand how it happened. There had to be some secret to explain it. The movie seemed to reflect that possession occurred in the air and was represented by people speaking in tongues or in non-native languages. I remember being worried about having the window open when I watched the movie by myself at night. I was relatively unafraid of it. I lived with the devil:

'Cause I have wandered through this world

And as each moment has unfurled

I've been waiting to awaken from these dreams

People go just where they will

— Doctor My Eyes, Jackson Browne

I saw a Reiki worker, Dove, on August seventeenth, the day I was supposed to take my trip to Michigan to visit my family. I told my parents that I had COVID as an excuse. My father's response was that he was "disappointed." The woman immediately said that she believed I needed the energy cleansing and that I was ready to do the work. She connected to the different chakra centers of my body.

She started at my sacrum, my "will" center, and placed her hand under my hip. The Sacral Chakra is located just below your belly button. It's linked to creativity, emotions, and your ability to enjoy life. When this chakra is balanced, you feel joyful and open to new experiences. If it's out of balance, you might struggle with emotional issues or have trouble being creative. My sacrum released within thirty seconds.

Dove moved up to my heart area, and I told her that my heart felt vulnerable and exposed. The Heart Chakra is located in the center of your chest. It's all about love, compassion, and your ability to connect with others. When this chakra is open, you feel loving and connected, both to yourself and to other people. If it's blocked, you might struggle with feelings of isolation or have trouble forming close relationships. My body was trembling on and off during the exercise. I let my body tremble and adjust to the touch of her hands. I convulsed a series of times, and she told me to try a centering exercise. She asked me to put my left hand on my navel and my right thumb and pinky on the left and right sides of my collarbone. My breathing was shallow, and she told me to take deep belly breaths. I felt intense pain in the back of my ribs, as if someone was stabbing me in the back.

I told her that when I was twelve years old in sixth grade, I had repeated incidents where I would cough, my eyes would water, and I would need to leave the classroom. I finished my coughing fits in the restroom. I was incredibly triggered and irritated. I would yell out loud at my body, "Get it together! You're embarrassing me!" When we got to my throat chakra, I was coughing and expelling air. This is the chakra focused on finding your voice. It makes sense that this part of my energy was blocked. The Throat Chakra is linked to communication and self-expression. When this chakra is balanced, you can speak your truth clearly and effectively. If this chakra is blocked, you might find it hard to express your thoughts or feel misunderstood.

She asked me if I had ever had a craniectomy and noticed that there was a lot of energy around my head. She asked if he had physically assaulted me, and I said not that I was aware of, but I told her that I was starting to think that I was sexually abused. She shuddered in silent acknowledgment. The Crown Chakra is located at the top of your head. It's connected to spiritual connection and enlightenment. When this chakra is balanced, you feel a sense of peace and connection to the universe. It helps you feel connected to something greater than yourself. If it's blocked, you might feel disconnected or lack a sense of purpose.

She asked if I had ever done a cord-cutting exercise before. I said I had not, but that I would like to. She called in Archangel Gabriel and

Jesus Christ and said that all energy from my father needed to be released. I silently sobbed. She told Gabriel to come in with his sword, and I could feel the energy. Then she called in Jesus, and I could feel a warmth in my heart. It was an incredibly powerful and transformational experience that, in many ways, transcends the written word.

Afterward, she took me outside to perform an energy releasing exercise. She told me to sit with my hands outstretched and open and to say, "This is the energy in my body. My energy belongs to me! All other energy must go!" and to exhale loudly three times.

I had been no contact with my father for four weeks at that point, and he was slowly ramping up his tactics to get my husband's and my attention. He texted me with passive-aggressive comments about me ignoring his calls. He congratulated my husband on his ten-year anniversary in South Carolina, which was odd because this was posted on social media, and my father said he rarely used Facebook. He was suspicious that my mother and I were in contact because she loved her grandchildren more than anything. He said, "Maybe we won't have to make the twelve-hour drive to South Carolina anymore," waiting for her response. I knew he never cared about me, and it was nice to get that firsthand proof.

One evening, my father sent out a message to the group text saying, "Please confirm if you are in the hospital with Y or N." I was sobbing on the couch, so exhausted from his torment and feeling like I was still under his control twelve hours away. I told my husband to say "N," and

I told my mom that I could not keep the charade anymore. I was done pretending.

There was one especially traumatizing workday that changed the course of my life. My workday started relatively well. I told my coworker, Savannah, about the tension leaving my body and that I had taken up my cross for Christ. Savannah told me that her boyfriend was going through major difficulties; he was getting hiccups all the time. I said that this was related to his throat chakra, preventing him from speaking his truth. I suggested that he could listen to a chakra meditation while performing a grounding technique to assist with cleansing the throat chakra.

There was a birthday lunch get-together about ten minutes away. I was sleep-deprived, and it seemed that my left brain was not functioning at its highest capacity. My co-worker, Stephanie, left and said that she needed to let her dog out. She asked me to let her know when she was leaving. I was feeling triggered about making sure that I left on time, so I rushed out in my car to make it to the birthday lunch.

This was another trifecta of triggers: my birthdays were always ruined, I had terrible social anxiety due to the constant shaming by my father, and I had to drive to get there. My vehicle had built-in safety features, but I was too far in my right brain to understand the logic behind that. I rushed to try and make the luncheon on time; I sensed negative energy around me everywhere.

When I arrived at the luncheon, I tried to ground myself. I walked in and was told by my boss, Jeremy, "I'm not happy with you right now;

you're on my bad list." I told him that I was in survival mode and had no bandwidth to think about others.

He said he had tried calling me multiple times and that I did not answer my desk phone. He went on and on about how upset he was. I was smack dab in an emotional flashback, but I was too sleep-deprived for my left brain to kick on and assist with logic. I was my truest self — the self that I had to keep hidden in my subconscious in the business world to survive.

Next, our co-worker, who is incredibly self-involved and lacking in self-awareness, was nowhere to be found ten minutes after the start of the luncheon. She called Jeremy to ask him where we were. She accepted the meeting invite, so we were all baffled as to why she needed a verbal invitation. She finally showed up twenty minutes late. She seemed to think that it was somebody else's responsibility to take her there. She was the victim in any situation. This was very irritating to me, as I felt that the larger group's time was being wasted.

I left work mid-afternoon that day to go home. I work with three very large men, all over 6 feet tall, who remind me of my father and regularly, unintentionally invade my space, putting me in my fawn response. There are four potential trauma responses, and the responses get progressively more traumatized: fight, flight, freeze, and fawn. During my childhood, I could not fight, flee, or freeze, so I had to fawn ninety percent of the time. This trauma response is observable in nature, where animals literally play dead to prevent being eaten. These three men typically have differing priorities that put me smack dab in a fawn trauma response. I struggle to figure out whom to please and how to please them. I decided that I needed to say something to two of the men I trusted.

I called Scott, our Vice President of Operations, one late afternoon and was in a panic attack for most of the phone conversation. My father had told me repeatedly that I would be killed if I told my story, so it was incredibly triggering. I also had some lingering trauma in my lungs and rib area, which prevented me from taking a deep breath. My instincts were right; this co-worker said that he would try very hard not to trigger me in the future and added, "Thank you for sharing, and again, let me know if I am being a boob. If there is anything I can do to help, even if it's just giving you someone to beat up for a bit, I'm happy to assist." It felt great to be seen, felt, and heard.

Next, I called my boss, Jeremy, around 8 PM. I said, "I was sexually abused my entire childhood, and my father told me he would kill me if I ever said anything. My mother and brother are considering leaving him." I was in another panic attack. My boss was speechless and immediately validated my experience, to his immense credit. He could not believe that I had a childhood that traumatic and somehow came out relatively well-adjusted and resilient. I said that I knew he did not do it intentionally, but when he barged into my office, it could be very scary, and I jumped into the fawn trauma response. I also mentioned that the situation with one of our businesses getting sold was extra traumatizing for me because I was very close to a few of my coworkers, and it brought up my abandonment trauma. It felt like our work family — a family I chose — was being torn apart. My abandonment trauma was kicking in deep. I told him that my life's work had been centered on giving a voice to the voiceless. I had empathy for everyone else. Now was the time to give myself empathy and connect to my authentic self.

Jeremy was extremely empathetic. He said, "Knowing you, you are probably second-guessing yourself about whether you should have told me. You may question if I think less of you for telling me this. I do not think less of you for telling me; I think more of you. I will support you however you need; just let me know what that looks like." I regained an important part of my soul and my voice that day. The feeling of being supported felt incredible.

The next morning, I called my mother and talked to her about the Reiki body work. She asked where the kids were, and I told her that they were in the car with me. We got into a shouting match, where she started to gaslight me, and I said, "Talk to your therapist!" before hanging up the phone. Driving was a major trigger for me, given my history, and I did not have the mental or emotional bandwidth to mother her.

I liked to think I had at least one secure attachment from childhood with my mother, but that proved to be false. Toxic shame is a recurring theme within the history of both of my extended families and serves as a barrier to connecting with one's authenticity. My mother was too deep in her own toxic shame to be present for me as a mother. She internalized her mother's shame; you could tell this because she had the look of disgust when my grandmother would ask incessant questions about my brother and me when we were kids. It was the same face I presented when she asked for every detail about my kids. There was hidden resentment in being present for my kids in a way that she was never present for me.

My mother tried to project her resentment and shame onto me, but I was no longer taking on anyone else's energy. She called back repeatedly and said, "I don't think I deserved that!" I told her that I was not dealing with this anymore. She shouted, "NO!!!" This was not her voice; it was the voice of one of her parents — parents who never allowed her to defend herself. As a young child, she told me that her only reprieve was yelling at the top of her lungs into a pillow when she was sent to her room. That trauma was alive and well now when I tried to assert my independence. I was deep in an emotional flashback, and the workday had begun.

I texted Jeremy to tell him that I needed the day off. He was very supportive, which gave me the space to delve deeper into the darkest parts of my story. I tried to ground myself at my friend's house, rocking in her swing. I wrote a series of pages, but my intense fear of being killed pulled me deep into my traumatic abuse at the beginning of my life.

I was incredibly triggered when I received an especially traumatic memory from when I was eight. Everything with my father was transactional, the law of the Old Testament. He knew I wanted a dog so desperately; I had to give something of myself to get something. One time during my abuse, I peed myself, and he called me a "bitch" when I was so terrified that I peed on the floor. Later that summer, we got a

Lhasa Apso. I could feel this memory when I turned my left leg upwards, like that of a female dog. Of course, I was "bad" because of this and responsible for that behavior. I was in an emotional flashback while on the phone with my friend, asking her for the code to get into her house because I had to use the restroom.

I made the difficult decision to go no contact with my mother. I found that we both needed to heal individually before we could reconnect. This was a heartbreaking decision, but I prayed about it, and God communicated to me that I needed to temporarily rid myself of this relationship, as it was toxic for me and would slow my healing journey.

The look of disgust is a clear giveaway of someone's toxic shame. Instead of working through their own internal battle — something required of us as true Christians — many people externalize their toxic shame onto the child who reminds them of their own toxic shame in childhood. My beautiful femininity reminded my father of his incest with his mother. To rid himself of any responsibility, he had to project it all onto me. His internal disgust had to be externalized for him to rid himself of the shame associated with it.

I became a receptacle for my father's and uncle's toxic shame. Everything that made me beautiful and feminine was destroyed by their shame. Anytime they felt a sexual urge that disgusted them from their childhood, they externalized it onto my beautiful, sacred feminine body. Toys were given during these transactions as my reward, at the cost of my self-worth and dignity.

I know this because as I worked through the deepest levels of my grief, I had clear feminine wounds. My beautiful, sacred feminine energy was slowly and systematically destroyed. It was death by a thousand cuts — slow enough that it was hard to notice. My beautiful feminine hips that worshipped God were destroyed, removed of all movement. My hands, meant to praise God, were bound in slavery. My voice, intended to speak my truth, was silenced.

I knew everyone else had worth and value; I spent my working career fighting for it. Why was I somehow exempt from this? Wasn't this a defiance of God, if I was made with a specific purpose? I was not living my authentic life, the life God planned out for me.

I was deep in an emotional flashback, in a panic attack so extreme that I thought I was going to die. My father told me that he would kill me if I told my story, so my fawn response was alive and well as I unearthed the deepest, most psychologically damaging memories of my trauma. Didn't Mary feel this way when she was told a child would be born to her as a Virgin? This was the act of me bearing my cross for Christ, confronting the pain that seemed impossible to overcome (which is perfectly captured in Luke).

"25 Large crowds were traveling with Jesus, and turning to them he said: 26 'If anyone comes to me and does not hate father and mother, wife and children, brothers and sisters — yes, even their own life — such a person cannot be my disciple. 27 And whoever does not carry their cross and follow me cannot be my disciple.'"

— Luke 14: 25-27

A woman saw me in my friend's yard and called 911. I was sleep-deprived and deep in meditation with God. I thought that I was on the cross as Christ was, and I kept saying that the only person who could spare me from the evil of this world was Jesus. I kept shouting, "I belong to Jesus!" The first responders tried to push me down, and I yelled, "I do not consent!" because I felt like they were trying to hold me down to have sex with me, as had been the case so much during my childhood.

I was taken for evaluation at the local emergency room. I was extremely thirsty and sleep-deprived. As I went into the bathroom, I saw a sign for a human trafficking hotline and immediately realized that I had been human trafficked for my entire childhood. I intuitively knew that this was my story.

I talked to a psychiatrist and told him my situation. He said that there was methamphetamine in my system. I explained that I was taking fifteen milligrams of Adderall. I was transferred to the psychiatric unit, but I knew that I was born again and free. I sang "Hallelujah" when I was being transported. I received some medication to help me with sleep.

During my five-day stay at the psychiatric ward, I used it as an opportunity to get much-needed rest. There were significant times of tribulation and complete helplessness, but I had a window to the outside world that I used to connect with God. I had my Bible transported to my room. I met a gentleman named Roderick, with whom I instantly connected. I told him my story of sexual abuse, and he said that he was a Vietnam vet and used to have panic disorders. He told me that Psalm 91 was his favorite psalm for protection. I read it and wept:

"[1]Whoever dwells in the shelter of the Most High will rest in the shadow of the Almighty. [2]I will say of the LORD, 'He is my refuge and my fortress, my God, in whom I trust.' [3]Surely he will save you from the fowler's snare and from the deadly pestilence. [4]He will cover you with his feathers, and under his wings you will find refuge; his faithfulness will be your shield and rampart. [5]You will not fear the terror of night, nor the arrow that flies by day, [6]nor the pestilence that stalks in the darkness, nor the plague that destroys at midday. [7]A thousand may fall at your side, ten thousand at your right hand, but it will not come near you. [8]You will only observe with your eyes and see the punishment of the wicked. [9]If you say, 'The LORD is my refuge,' and you make the Most High your dwelling, [10]no harm will overtake you, no disaster will come near your tent. [11]For he will command his angels concerning you to guard you in all your ways; [12]they will lift you up in their hands, so that you will not strike your foot against a stone. [13]You will tread on the lion and the cobra; you will trample the great lion and the serpent. [14]'Because he loves me,' says the LORD, 'I will rescue him; I will protect him, for he acknowledges my name. [15]He will call on me, and I will answer him; I will be with him in trouble, I will deliver him and honor him. [16]With long life I will satisfy him and show him my salvation.'"

— Psalm 91:1-16

I met Roderick for a reason and knew that my stay at the ward had a higher purpose. I was hoping to be able to leave one day but received the unfortunate news that I needed to stay one more day. I broke down like the helpless child who had been bound in physical and psychological slavery during her childhood. I screamed, "This is a living hell! How would you like to sleep on this bed? My back is killing me!"

The doctors assisting me said that they understood my frustration. I sobbed in my room, took a shower, and went to the nurses' station.

"I want to take a sleeping pill to get through the rest of this day," I said.

The unempathetic nurse replied, "We can't do that. It's too early. You're going home tomorrow anyway; what's the big deal?"

She was viewing me as less than human. I was being treated like an animal, and I longed to be set free. Once I gathered my strength and composure, I went back to my room, did some yoga exercises to calm my nerves, and silently said, "This is the day that the Lord has made. I will rejoice and be glad in it." That evening, I slept better. I was transported to a quieter unit where I could be discharged and processed more quickly.

That morning, I met a young woman who had a severe sexual abuse history. I gave her my phone number, email address, and mailing address. I knew that the extra day I was given to stay there had meaning and purpose. Waiting patiently, I went back to my room and let my deeper level trauma release from my body as I "trembled" before the Lord.

The woman who processed my belongings had a beautiful picture in her office. I asked where it was taken, and she told me that it was at Pretty Place, the location where I was married. I got goosebumps. God was truly looking out for me, and He was present.

When the nurse took my vitals that morning, my oxygen was at one hundred percent. I could finally take in full cleansing breaths. My chains were gone, and I had been set free.

There was an issue with the pharmacy regarding my discharge paperwork, which extended my stay. There was a man who kept giving me predatory eyes and was extremely triggering. I walked around the unit back and forth to release some of my pent-up energy. I finally realized that there was a brick I could stand behind so he was out of my view. I asked my nurse if I could go back to my room, and the last little bits of trauma left my body.

I was called in and walked out to the man of my dreams, my husband, who took on the job of loving me unconditionally — the way that I always sought to be loved. He was Christ-like, and I was now in my own heaven on earth. This period of darkness lasted twelve days, the number of God's perfection.

I am free. I am dancing with Jesus the way that my truest authentic self used to do. Nobody can keep me from my true authenticity if I am fearless enough to pursue it, just as God pursued me. As Psalm 34:14 states: "Turn from evil and do good; seek peace and pursue it."

I never belonged to my father or anyone; I have always and will always be God's child.

Part IV: Cultivating A Relationship With God

"Then Jesus declared, "I am the bread of life. Whoever comes to me will never go hungry, and whoever believes in me will never be thirsty."

— John 6:36, NIV

The following practices have been instrumental in my faith journey. My hope is that they prove to be beneficial to you.

1. **Dear Sisters, use a daily devotional to connect with God.** There are a multitude of apps you can download for free. I downloaded the Bible app. I like to start my morning by connecting with my daily Bible verse. My day is centered around the daily bread that God has provided for me. I truly believe my daily verse is handcrafted for me by God; He is relaying a message to me that I will be able to understand and contextualize. When I fail to live up to the command that God asks of me, I speak with Him in silence and apologize.

   My relationship with God is the most important relationship in my life. I have realized that I do not work for my boss anymore; I work for God. He is the ultimate decision maker in my life. He guides my decision-making, my words, and my thoughts.

   My daily Bible verse today was, "Very truly I tell you, whoever hears my word and believes him who sent me has eternal life and will not be judged but has crossed over from death to life" — John 5:24, NIV.

I feel His presence everywhere. I see Him as the fluffy clouds float above me while I lay in my hammock. I feel His warmth in the sun. I see His beauty in the beautiful mums I just bought for my front porch or the fox walking through the woods outside my office. I feel the Holy Spirit in the comfort of a cool breeze. I taste His nourishment in a fresh apple from an orchard. I hear Him when the song "Hallelujah" plays while I'm getting a massage or when a friend tells me a message that I need to hear.

I also like to start my day with praise music. The uplifting music helps me to see that God is everywhere and is always working with me to achieve my life's purpose. I have been very interested in Cory Asbury, Brandon Lake, KING & COUNTRY, and NEEDTOBREATHE lately. I listen to music with messages talking about the new life I have in Christ and the beauty of everyday life. My life's purpose now is to show other people His existence.

2. **Dear Sisters, do not take on other people's energy.** As a super empath, I tend to get lost in other people's energy. I want to help and fix things for them. This is not my job; only God can change their actions. My job is to show them God through my actions. If you feel like you are taking on other people's energy regularly, do this simple practice: stand with your arms outstretched and say, "This is my energy. My energy belongs to ME. All other energy must go!" Then take three large exhales.

I have taken up the daily practice of physically washing my hands to symbolize the ending of a thought or discussion on a particular subject. For example, I will wash my hands at the end of the workday to signify that I am done with the energy associated with the workday and can transition into my family time with my husband and children. I also use this ritual when I have made the decision to no longer entertain a relationship with a toxic person, which takes us into my next point.

3. **Dear Sisters, do not be afraid to rid yourself of toxic people.**

This concept is founded in Biblical scripture: "Do not be misled: 'Bad company corrupts good character. Come back to your senses as you ought, and stop sinning; for there are some who are ignorant of God — I say this to your shame.'"

— 1 Corinthians 15:33-34

For me to heal, I had to cut all ties with my father and mother. I used to think that removing family members from your life was not in accordance with God's commandments. I was brought up to "Honor thy father and mother" (this was my father's favorite go-to phrase whenever I had an opinion). I do not think that my father will ever seek out God. He has made it known to my mother that he does not believe in God. God only knows if that will happen. I still hold out hope that my mother and I will eventually reconnect. But it's not my job to tell her to leave an abusive relationship; that is ultimately her choice, her God-ordained free will.

If you have relationships that pull you away from God, suck all your energy, and perpetually make you feel bad about yourself, I recommend that you reduce your time with that person or potentially cut him or her out of your life altogether. I text my brother to get updates about the situation with him and my mother. My mother is sending my children's Bible to me later this week in the mail. I know that she is a God-fearing woman, so I appeal to this side of her spirit. But I have to limit contact as I continue to go through the deep healing. I do not want to stay stuck in the past; I want to see the beauty that is in my life now. I can relive my childhood through the lives of my children. Life is hard enough without people who constantly bring you down.

4. **Dear Sisters, if you have significant pain in your body, consider somatic work. Listen to the dialogue of your body.**

I have personally found yoga, guided meditation, and Reiki to be the most beneficial. There is a book titled *The Body Keeps the Score* that posits that our memories and emotions are trapped in our body. If you have significant pain in an area of your body, you most likely have stored trauma. The first step in processing any trauma is establishing safety. If your body is stuck in survival mode, the trauma will stay stuck. My journey started with a weekly yoga class. Moving your body will alert you to areas that are in pain. The pain in your body is a dialogue. For example, my stored trauma in my shoulders and neck held the memories of subjugation from my father. I worked through this trauma slowly, over the course of more than a year. As an anxious person, I have a tendency to hold my breath. I have a centering dove pendant that I hold on to, reminding me to take deep breaths. The guided meditations helped my right hemisphere come online and spark my creative energy. My Reiki session cleansed my body of all my father's energy — the terrible, harsh inner critic that I internalized from his intense abuse over the course of my childhood. Make sure any Reiki practitioner is a Christian; there are many gimmicks out there. The Reiki instructor should also be familiar with the seven chakras in the body, which I will discuss in more detail shortly.

Your gut instinct and your intuition are signs that something is off. Our gut is called our second brain due to the power it has in sending messages to us. Trust your gut and trust your God-given intuition. Our intuition is one of a woman's greatest gifts. Trust yourself. Trust your memories if they come up. The worst thing you can do is gaslight yourself about your story.

5. **Dear Sisters, be kind to yourself and others.** Everyone is fighting an internal battle. All habits become exponentially more ingrained over time — good begets good, evil begets evil. Research shows that habits develop after around thirty days of repeated practice. There is a book called *Atomic Habits: An Easy and Proven Way to Build Good*

Habits and Break Bad Ones by James Clear that I recommend. I used to be an extremely negative person. I have a scathingly harsh inner critic. I had to police myself in order to heal. If I had a negative thought, I would replace it with a positive one. I also have a tendency to gossip about other people. This does nothing to benefit me, the other person, or my Christian mission. I try to catch myself before I take the short pleasure in tearing someone else down. It is a struggle, but it is something I am working on. Another area is swearing. I used to have a terrible mouth. I would watch this around my children and still curse at work. But James talks about this in James 1:26-27: "Those who consider themselves religious and yet do not keep a tight rein on their tongues deceive themselves, and their religion is worthless. Religion that God our Father accepts as pure and faultless is this: to look after orphans and widows in their distress and to keep oneself from being polluted by the world."

If we are kind to ourselves, we can create space to be kind to others. I try to provide genuine words of encouragement. Everyone you encounter is fighting an unspoken battle. Every interaction you have with people is an opportunity for you to show them the Holy Spirit that lives in you. With regular practice, you will find that this becomes second nature. Goodness and kindness are a daily choice — our God-given free will.

6. **Dear Sisters, connect with the seven deadly sins and identify which ones you are most susceptible to, and combat them with the seven heavenly virtues that counteract them. Learn which of your seven chakras are blocked and cleanse them**

The seven deadly sins are those sins that spur all other sins and further immoral behavior. First enumerated by Pope Gregory I (the Great) in the 6th century and elaborated upon in the 13th century by St. Thomas Aquinas, they are (1) pride, (2) greed,

(3) lust, (4) envy, (5) gluttony (which is usually understood to include drunkenness), (6) wrath, and (7) sloth. Each of these can be overcome with the seven heavenly virtues of (1) humility, (2) charity, (3) chastity, (4) gratitude, (5) temperance, (6) patience, and (7) diligence.

The deadly sin that I most identify with is pride. I believe that I can do everything on my own and hate depending on others. I have a tendency to think that I have all the answers or that I am smarter than others. This is not being Christ-like.

To counteract this, I need to remember to be humble, the virtuous opposite of pride. I need to ask for help, as I have slowly learned to do during my healing journey. I need to keep my ego in check. I need to submit to my husband if he shows me unconditional love. Above all else, I need to submit to the will of God. We all have an internal battle of God versus evil. Each person has one, and it is a daily struggle. I am inspired by the words of Paul in Philippians 4:13: "I can do all this through him who gives me strength."

We, as Christians, are the body of Christ in human form. It is beautiful to achieve communion with others. If you are struggling, reach out; go to a church even if you are utterly broken and don't feel like it. The music and meditation will appeal to your subconscious self, your shadow. This is the time when God needs you the most.

During this period of repentance and healing, you will ask if God can take your pain away. The easiest way for me to work through this is to listen to praise music on Spotify and to pray repetitively. You know best what self-soothing techniques are most beneficial to you. Sins are a way to keep us apart from God in a different reality altogether, kept in the law of the Old Testament that is transcended in the New Testament with Christ's sacrifice.

The number seven appears more than fifty times in the Bible and is associated with holiness and perfection. There are:

- Seven days of creation
- Seven days of the week
- Seven deadly sins
- Seven deadly virtues
- Seven chakras

To ascend to a true higher level of consciousness, we are called to confront the burdens of our body (our traumas) and work through them to understand our higher purpose. This can be achieved through the seven chakras. Chakras are seven energy centers of the body. Connecting with your chakras connects you to your spiritual self. Blocked chakras can lead to pain and block you from your life's purpose and authenticity.

Chakras are not mentioned in the Bible, but there is a word, Ruach, a Hebrew term used repeatedly throughout the Bible that means "breath of God." This energy is first mentioned in the second verse of the Bible.

"Now the earth was formless and empty, darkness was over the surface of the deep, and the Spirit of God was hovering over the waters."

— Genesis 1:2

The Holy Spirit is referred to in detail during the New Testament. Jesus is filled with the Spirit when he is tempted by the devil in Luke 4:

"Jesus, full of the Holy Spirit, left the Jordan and was led by the Spirit into the wilderness, where for forty days he was tempted by the devil. He ate nothing during those days, and at the end of them he was hungry."

Peter talks about the Spirit as he and the other disciples spread the Gospel after Jesus's crucifixion in Acts 2:38-39:

"38Peter replied, 'Repent and be baptized, every one of you, in the name of Jesus Christ for the forgiveness of your sins. And you will receive the gift of the Holy Spirit. 39The promise is for you and your children and for all who are far off—for all whom the Lord our God will call.'"

7. **Dear Sisters, find your version of heaven and pursue it**
   My version of heaven is nature. I feel like I am in my own Eden again. I am amazed at the beauty of the natural world. I love to sit outside and admire the splendor all around me. I feel like I have been remade through this trial in Christ, as if I have been born again in my own version of Eden. I now exist in this heaven on earth. Your version of heaven reflects your inner child during your most authentic self.

I'm splashing in puddles at four years old as the rain falls on me, without care for how wet I am getting. I am twirling in circles, my arms outstretched, heart open to God because I know of God's promise in the rainbow breaking through the clouds.